# ESCAPE

# How to beat the Narcissist

# BY

# H G TUDOR

# Escape

## How to Beat the Narcissist

## By

## H G Tudor

Published by Insight Books

## Dedications

To those who gathered the strength to fight back.

To those determined to escape.

# Introduction

Where are you right now? I do not mean where are you sat reading this book, at home or travelling on the tube to work. I mean where are you at? Have you discovered that you are in the maelstrom of a narcissistic whirlwind? Most likely. You may have taken years to reach this point of realisation. You have known for a long time that something is not right but you have not been able to put your finger on what is causing it. Instead, as the empath that attracted us, you have spent your time trying to weather the storm, to sooth and placate and to try and understand. After all this time you have finally gained an insight into the beast you have danced the exhausting dance with all these years. The creature that has leeched from you in every conceivable manner and then given nothing back.

You fell in love with the heaven sent individual, man or woman. They lit up your life and made everything shine and sparkle. You may have been suffering in some way but they picked you up and dusted you down and made you feel so special, so wonderful and so loved. That faded a long time ago and yet you still stayed, clinging onto the hope that you could return to that golden period and make everything alright again.

Thus where are you now? Beaten, battered and bruised. Exhausted, shattered and drained. You cannot think straight. You are sapped of your strength and your energy. You never see your friends and hardly ever your family. You are isolated and trapped in this hellish false reality that I have created. It is a monumental effort for you to climb out of your bed and get through the day. You just want to be left alone. You want it to stop but it will not. The demonic merry-go-round spins faster and faster and you can feel yourself fading away.

You are now reading the answer. I am a narcissist. I know my kind and what goes on in our minds. I know how we behave, think and react and I am going to provide this knowledge to you to enable you to escape and beat your narcissist.

I suspect that when you read "How to beat the narcissist" you immediately said to yourself, "with a club". Many of you, with some justification, will feel that way. Satisfying as it may be to stove in the head of the narcissist who has plagued your life spending time in prison would actually provide us with the last laugh.

Instead of advocating a violent approach to eradicate us, this book is aimed at enabling you to escape the worst of our behaviours. You are fully familiar with our abusive ways as you have been on the receiving end of many of them for a long time. Some you may be aware of and others you have learned are much more insidious. Sometimes you may not even be able to link the way you feel with how we treat you. On other occasions it is as obvious and as brutal as a punch in the mouth.

The purpose of this book is to offer you advice from someone who is very much in the know. There are many books written by those who have been through the horrendous experience of having had a relationship with a narcissist. Many are completely unaware of what they have been put through until a well-informed friend or a professional has told them, or they have read one of my other publications, which has put them firmly in the picture.

Others are still ensnared in the narcissist's clutches. They may lack the emotional strength and force of will to get away from the narcissist. They are not yet equipped to make that break and therefore need assistance in managing the manipulative behaviour of the narcissist to diminish or extinguish his or her toxic effect.

Alternatively, getting completely away from the narcissist may not realistically be an option, notwithstanding the strength of will and purpose that the individual may have. It may be very difficult for them to do so as the narcissist is their boss, a family member or they share parenting duties with the narcissist.

The golden rule in evading the continuing clutches of a narcissist is to go no contact. It is sound advice. Nothing infuriates us more than being ignored. When this happens, the vast majority of us will then lose interest in you. It is too difficult to extract any fuel from you and as I have mentioned on previous occasions we do not like to expend our energy unnecessarily. Accordingly, we will move on and seek out new sources of fuel which are far easier to extract from. There are plenty around. A handful of my kind may still pursue you even if you apply the approach of no contact. Those are my malign brethren whose ultimate aim is your destruction. In those instances, you are left with little choice but to either move a long way away (I am talking countries or continents) and/or utilising the power of the law to protect yourself. The malign of our variety will continue to pursue you unless restrained from doing so.

Of course, if no contact was the answer to every situation then this would be a short book indeed. No contact may be an eventual aim or it may not be something that can be achieved. What you need instead is to know how to manage the manipulative techniques that we narcissists deploy in order to minimise their impact on you and thus escape their effect. This might be to enable you to muster sufficient strength to leave us and apply no contact or it may be so that you can regain some control in your life when you have no option but to continue to have involvement with us. As mentioned above, there are many people who advise on how to deal with a narcissist's manipulative wiles on a day by day basis, based on their own experience or from repeated studying of narcissists from a professional perspective. Those books are very good and are full of useful ideas and techniques indeed.

This book provides you with counter techniques from the perspective of a narcissist. Nobody knows how effective these techniques are on our kind, as our kind. I know full well the impact and I also allow you to understand how it has such an impact to satisfy your craving, as an empath, for answers. Receiving this information from a practitioner of the dark art of narcissism is akin to being granted unfettered access to a gold mine.

You have the added advantage of knowing that it works (I am telling you that it does) but also of how it impacts on me. If revenge is your thing, you are able to garner a slice of it by knowing the effect these steps will have on me. Not all have an effect. Many are about self-preservation and nullifying my effect. In certain instances, the counter techniques can be applied to several different types of related manipulative actions. The intention of this is that if you know what you are dealing with, since you have read my book **Manipulated** which shows you twenty-five manipulative techniques we narcissists use, then this will provide you with suggestions to counter those tactics. Thus, it can be read in conjunction with **Manipulated** or as a stand alone once you know the behaviours you are dealing with.

You should be accustomed by now to my direct and no-nonsense approach. There is no time to indulge in the science here, no matter how interesting this is and it is not my expertise that is for others to advise you about.

You need help and you need it fast. This is where you find it.

# Mindset

The fundamental step you need to take to escape my kind and me is to alter your mindset. People like you (and by that I mean honest, decent and caring people) know you are being abused. You tend to know quite soon you are being abused although you often do not realise that you are being subject to certain insidious manipulative techniques. That is why my book **Manipulated** is very important in giving you a wake up call.

What you must understand is that we know you recognise you are being abused. We also know that you have no idea (often for along time) that your abuser is one of us; a narcissist. We also know that there is a long list of reasons why you will not do anything about it. Yes, I know it sounds incredible when you read it like that but it is a fact. You are an intelligent, observant and decent person who is being subjected to awful abuse and you still hang around and allow yourself to be subjected to it. You may not be aware of all the forms of abuse you are being subjected to, but you know that somebody striking you is abusive, you know being shouted at and called a rotten, worthless whore is abusive and you know that being locked out of your house because you chose to go and see your friends for once in a blue moon is abusive. Yet you do nothing. Why?

- Finance

- Children

- History together

- You feel obliged to care for me because I have a different illness

- Family pressure

- Mortgage

- Shame

- Hope – you are addicted to the potential that things might get better

- Conditioning

- The intensity of my Love Bombing

- Fear (of my reaction, of being alone)

- Denial – this is not really happening to me

- Pride

- Change is hard

- You want the relationship to succeed

- You don't mind the relationship being so lopsided because you are a giver

- I am broken and you want to fix me

The list is long and I am sure you can add many more reasons to the few I have just listed by example there. You know all these reasons. Guess what? So do I. In fact, a number of them I engineered. I made you codependent on me. I ensured that financially you are shafted if you left me. I have made you feel guilty about splitting up and the effect it might have on the children. All of this has been carefully thought out to ensure that there are as many obstacles both physical, financial, emotional and psychological to you being able to escape me. You may well have looked down that list and ticked every single one and then sank back into your chair and decided you are sunk. You will never escape. You are trapped in my hell until one of us dies.

That is what I am a counting on. In order to control you, I have to subjugate you and I do that by extinguishing any hope that you may have that you may escape from me. If you do not think you can, there is no possibility of you even attempting it is there? I have made it so hard for you, it will be easier for you to pick one of the reasons above and stick with it. In fact, you will convince yourself that it is easier to endure the daily torment of abuse that I inflict on you than it is to escape it. Read that last sentence again. It makes no sense does it? Yet that is exactly what you are doing. I know all of this and I love it.

Yet I am going to tell you how you can escape me. It can be done. You may escape all of me or if that is not feasible (for reasons I expand on below and especially in the section on no contact) then you can at least escape the worst of my abusive and manipulative behaviours by adopting the advice I provide.

The first and most important step however is that you must want to escape. To achieve that state of mind you need to list all of the reasons you can think of as to why you cannot escape. Take your time. Finesse the list. Check it over. Then I want you to read through that list one last time. Next, take a pen and write next to each reason the words "Stay abused or". Write that phrase five, ten or how many other times you have reasons written down. For each of those reasons you can stay being abused or you can do something about it. Which is worse? Finding a solution or staying abused? Precisely. You then must not move until you have written down the solution alongside the "stay abused or". There is a solution. There is an alternative for each one. They may not be easy but they exist, but they are easier than being subjected to me for the rest of your life.

I could offer you some suggestions as how to tackle those reasons for staying but I am not going to. That is not my role (and after all I am not going to give you all the answers, that would not be any fun) but you have it within you to work it all out. You don't need the detail, just the broad brush answer. When people decide to solve a country's major problems they do not have the detail ready to begin with. Not at all. What they do have is the statement of intent and what they want to achieve. They then go and work it out. You will do that. You have your statements of intent and that means you want to change your mindset, you have changed your mindset. You now have the beginning of a plan to overcome all those reasons for staying within my abusive world. Now what you need is advice about how to deal with me.

Oddly enough I am an expert in me so you are going to benefit from the diamond grade material that I am going to furnish you with in order to escape what me and my kind do to you. I will take you through a range of manipulative techniques that I use and how you can look to escape their effect on you.

# A Broken Machine

One theme that I make repeated mention of is how your innate goodness and empathic nature proves to be your downfall with my kind and me. It may not be a permanent downfall hence the purpose of this book. Your core beliefs made you susceptible to our seduction. Your desire to aid, help and assist results in your being exactly what makes our manipulation of you so effective. People without your admirable attributes are not ensnared by us. They are not attractive to us in the beginning and even if they were, they would sense something is not right about us, act on that gut instinct and evade us. They may not work out exactly what we are, but they will recognise and act on their instincts.

Fortunately for us, you do not. You invariably have no idea what we are up to as you succumb to our love bombing. If you have an inkling that something is not right, you will brush it aside in order to keep our affection and love. You also give people the benefit of the doubt. It is both a strength and a weakness. You want to see the good in everyone. Ultimately, you are a firm believer that love conquers all. Your dedication to caring, being a good and decent person means we seduce you, you remain as we abuse you and you are dangled on a string back and forth as we discard you and then pull you back in looking to extract more droplets of fuel from you.

One of the things that keeps you hanging on and coming back is the hope of returning to the golden period. You must realise that it was an illusion. It felt real, it seemed real but it was not. We give you glimpses of this heaven from time to time to lower your defences and suck you back in but we either never deliver it again or if we do it is only for a short period of time. It can only be for a short period of time because it is false and we do not have the energy or capability to maintain the pretence for long, not when our energies must be applied in the never ending pursuit of our fuel.

The second thing that keeps you hanging on and coming back is the delusion that we can change. This appeals so much to your core belief in fixing things and making them better. We may tell you we want to be a better person, we may convince you that this time, things will be different (even though this is the sixth time you have heard us say this) and we say sorry and we will try harder. You love to hear this. It is vindication that your perseverance has paid off. Your dogged tenacity and unshakeable belief in us will pay off. You truly believe that. You do not want plaudits for having made us a better person. That is not your style. You just want to be happy. You want both of us to be happy. Together.

This cannot ever and will never happen. We are broken beyond repair. We are a machine that is damaged and will only function in one way; to extract fuel from you at any cost to you without any concern for the consequence or effect it may have on your sanity, well-being, psyche, finances, physical health or self-esteem. Our selfishness is such that we will bite deep and suck deep as we look to extract as much fuel as we can from you. We will pore over your broken remains looking for a few drips to feed our insatiable hunger. When you have respite from us and have recovered to some degree, we appear again ready to gorge on you a further time. This is what we exist for. We are not open to change. We are not able to change. We do not want to change. You cannot fix us. Do not try as you will only fail.

Thus you must always keep in mind the following: -

1.   The golden period was an illusion

2.   It will never return in any permanent form

3.   We cannot be fixed

4.   We will not change

5.   We are destroyers

Do this as you apply these techniques and tactics and never let these five points stray far from your mind.

# Us

I have explained five points which you should keep in mind about our general nature and your mind set as you read this book. I also need to convey to you that in order to escape the effect of our nefarious behaviours you need to understand two fundamental things about my kind and me with regard to *why we act as we do.*

I could go into considerable detail here explaining to you how I have become what I am, that I was neglected as a child or that I was smothered with being made to feel special during my childhood. I might recount tales about the influence of a narcissistic parent and engage in protracted introspection to assist you in gaining an understanding of how I became the creature I am. That is not going to help you. By all means, if you are interested in understanding what made us what we are, there is plenty of literature. I would recommend you save that until you have made your escape or limited my influence, when you have room to breathe once again. You can then indulge yourself in learning all about how my treatment in my formative years caused me to become the beast that I am now. Furthermore, I am not prone to that type of introspection so I am not going to share it with you and in any event, understanding all of that will not help you escape me.

No, the key is not understanding how I was formed. The key is not even to understand why I do everything that I do. The key is to understand that you cannot understand. This is a difficult lesson for someone like you but it is a fundamental one.

You need to have an answer for everything. As a caring, honest empath, you want to understand how people work so you can better help them. It is a laudable concept and one I wholly endorse for without it, you would not be the prime providers of fuel that we need (more on that in a moment). You have to understand why people do things. You like that order. You like cause and effect. You need to be able to see that x happened because of y and does this present you with an opportunity to help in any way? If you are not able to understand why something is happening, this strikes at your very being. You find it confusing, unsettling and disturbing. You will try your damnedest to gain that understanding, even if in the process you harm yourself.

I will provide a brief example. I have shouted and ranted at you because you have failed to collect my suit from the dry cleaners. I accuse you of disrespecting me through this behaviour. This reaction on my part leaves you utterly perplexed. Why is this?

1. I had said I was going to collect the suit;

2. The suit can still be collected from the dry cleaners as it has not yet closed

3. Even if you had forgotten to pick it up, how is this disrespecting me?

4.  Even if you cannot get the suit, I do not need it immediately.

You have applied logic to the scenario.

I do not. I want to manipulate you and draw fuel from you. To do this I need to provoke a reaction from you. If I apply logic, this will not work, so I apply anti-logic and lose my temper with you knowing that you will not understand how someone normal could lose their temper in this way. This will cause you to argue back, possibly cry or look to placate me in some other way. Thus you give me a reaction and you give me fuel.

That is what we bring about in you. We want you confused and disorientated. We want you striving to get the answers so you question us, try and help us and plead with us to talk to you about what is really bothering us. This keeps you latched on to us and supplies us with fuel.

You must understand that we do not deal in logic.

I will write that again.

You must understand that we do not deal in logic.

There is no reason to our behaviour **in your reality**. Our conduct and our words make perfect sense in our twisted reality, but in your world they do not.  The sooner you realise that you cannot understand why we do certain things then the sooner you have taken a massive step towards escaping our malign influences.  Not only will you gain the understanding that our behaviour makes no sense in your reality you will also no longer feel the need to try and understand and thus you are setting yourself free from applying all that energy in pursuit of a useless conclusion. You have instantly removed a layer of confusion and anxiety. The energy you have saved can be far better applied to preserving your sense of self and applying the techniques I detail below to avoiding the effect of our manipulative behaviour.

Thus, in reading everything below always keep in your mind that we are not practitioners in logic, we are practitioners in energy. Know and recognise that and you have just taken a huge step forward in escaping my kind and me. This now leads me on to my second point.

We want fuel. We want supply from you. This is in the form of attention and reaction. We are always hungry for this fuel. It dominates our thoughts from the moment we wake until the moment we sleep. It is what we are put on this earth to obtain. We must have it. The way we obtain it is to apply our array of manipulative techniques to then cause a reaction in you. If you shout, scream, cry, hit us, call us names, sob, plead, placate, soothe, buy us gifts, run around after us, submit to us, bend over backwards and splay yourselves before us you are giving us a reaction and thus we get fuel from you.

You cannot possibly understand how important this fuel is to us because you are not one of us. Do not trouble yourself with trying to understand how someone could possibly spend all of their time dedicated to such a task. There is no point. You cannot understand this so do not bother. Do not waste your energy. Instead, know this is what we want.

Understand we have to have it and we will get it from you. In order to escape us, you need to learn not to provide us with this fuel.

Accordingly, the two fundamental points you need to keep in your mind in respect of why we behave as we do, as you read through this book and then apply its principles thereafter are as follows: -

1　We deal in energy not logic;

2　We want you to fuel us.

You are now cracking the code to escape us.

# The Power of Ignore

I

Hate

Being

Ignored

I am going to start you off with the thermonuclear weapon that you have in your armoury to escape my machinations. The power to ignore me. This is the silver bullet, the crucifix to the heart, the water over the wicked witch of the west. I love attention. I love attention in all its many forms, both positive and negative. I want you to admire me, talk about me, point me out, cry over me, laugh about me, speak to me, shout at me, hit me and kiss me. Give me the attention. Show me the attention.

Deprive me of attention and you immediately remove my fuel. Be warned, I will apply every manipulative technique I have learned and lash out in order to resume that supply of fuel. I have to have it and by ignoring me you have dramatically and instantly stopped it. It hurts. Oh it hurts so much. I have nothing now which I can use to maintain my façade and shield me from the reality. I do not want to see that reality. I must not see that reality. When you ignore me, you remove the fuel, the generator stops and the projector can no longer display what I wanted it to display and the wretched self that I am is visible to all the world and it wounds me so deeply and so badly that I have to slink away and curl up in a corner hoping I vanish. So awful is that sensation that is why we crave your attention and why you must not ignore us. If you do so we will fight hard, damn hard to win your attention once again. Anything to avoid the reality.

Babies need attention. Their cry is designed to jar your senses within a second so that you will attend to them. Babies are narcissists. Feed me, clean me, cuddle me, keep me warm and so on. They are attention magnets and they are designed to be the focus of all your attention. Of course as time goes on, the baby becomes a toddler and starts to give something back to you for all that time and attention you have invested in him or her. I have seen some of it in my nieces and nephews but moreover have been bored stupid by the tales from my siblings of the first smile, the first laugh, the cuddles and the first word. The delight you obtain from the unconditional love that you receive from these little beings as they begin to crawl and then take their first steps. You are receiving love, affection and enduring memories.

You get none of that from me. Yes, I know that we are likened to babies. The experts talk about how our emotional development has been arrested and that is why we are stuck in childhood with regard to our demands and responses. I do not agree with all of that. As I have just explained, you get something back from children. You get nothing good from my kind and me. Oh of course at first you do, but soon after all you receive from us are pain, heart ache, abuse, agony and wretchedness. No child does that do they?

We are akin to the helpless child as we desperately need your attention. (We are not interested in love or being liked, we want your admiration and attention) accordingly, to liken us to the sweet-smell and the heavenly laughter of a child is erroneous.

If you ignore me I start to shrivel and wither. Yes, I will fight against it and try my upmost to get you to engage with me through all manner of my manipulative techniques but if you can learn to ignore me then you have a very good chance of escaping my clutches. Ignoring me comes in different forms. There is the holy grail of ignoring me, no contact and I discuss that further. Of course, for reasons I will also expand on, no contact is not always an option. Accordingly, you need to apply ignoring me in a different way. You need to ignore my insults, ignore my temper tantrums, ignore my slurs to other people or ignore my silent treatment of you. By applying your power to ignore to a multiplicity of situations you will maintain calm and control whilst undermining me and denying the very power source that I crave. Apart from the most determined and malign of our kind, the frequent use of ignoring us will cause us to go elsewhere for our fuel. You are no longer providing it and it is far too hard to extract it from you. You will have escaped us. Those of us who show more determination will continue in our pursuit to extract fuel from you and also crush you. You need to apply the power to ignore in those situations to minimise our power over you and also to diminish the effect of our unpleasant behaviour on you.

Be under no illusion (oh the irony of that phrase) your Power to Ignore is your trump card but maintaining it is very difficult. It is easy to start and so hard to finish. Think of a baby crying. How difficult is that to ignore? Even if it is not your child or is not even a relative, a baby crying near you puts you on edge. You want it stop. You need to find a way to bring the horrible crying to an end and that is by giving him or her attention.

We are the same. Stop giving us attention and listen to us wail. We will throw tantrums, break things, call you names, ply you with guilt, assassinate your character to others, triangulate and so on and so on as we pick another manipulative method from our tool box. We have many tools and we will try them all as we know, most of the time, you will buckle and give us what we want. Attention. You may apologise. You may cry. You may shout or give us a hug. It does not matter what form it takes as long as it is attention. Thus you need to ensure you have the energy available to maintain your Power to Ignore. Conserve that energy, remove anything that drains it which is not productive and then channel it to this power. Like Captain Kirk sending all power to the front deflector shield, you need to be able to have enough energy to make this formidable weapon work.

Consequently, in all your dealings with my behaviour, in all the recommendations that I make for you in the coming pages, always keep as watchword to your heart your power to ignore. It will serve you well. It is often hard to maintain. We know this. You are not the type of person who finds ignoring someone or their behaviour a natural thing to do. You like to engage with people, you thrive on interaction with people and you like to give your time, love and attention to people. This of course should only be given to those who merit it. We think we do, very much so, but we do not. For you however, you are programmed to engage and we are aware of it, that is why we will fight hard not to be ignored in the hope that you will eventually give in. Like the child sulking in a corner until it is allowed to play out, we will keep going in the hope that your pleasant nature will ride your will power and you will eventually give in. Do not. Stay strong. Stay focussed and unleash your power to ignore.

# Methods of Escape

Having set the scene and adjusted your mind set, having ensured you are keeping in mind the two key fundamentals for dealing with us and having reminded you to conserve your energy you are ready to digest the various ways in which you can escape our behaviours. I have chosen a number of manipulative techniques that we apply. Most will be familiar to you. I detail, from my perspective what you can do to minimise and thus escape their effects. The advantage of this is that not only will this result in you feeling calmer, less anxious and stronger, it will mean you have more energy to apply to more techniques and it should therefore cause your strength to snowball and allow greater relief from us.

We will of course fight back. You will not have it all one way. It is not a case of being able to turn the tide and rout us from the battlefield. No, there will be further battles, long and bloody and the war will ebb and flow, but by paying heed to my message you will eventually find you are escaping my kind and mine's behaviour more and more.

In some instances, with the less powerful of my brethren this may have the happy effect of causing them to give up on you and leave you alone by seeking out weaker individuals and applying their techniques to them instead. We love control and if we sense it is weakening we will try and reassert it. If this is difficult or expends too much of our energy, we will leave you alone and go and find our fuel elsewhere. We may of course come back but you will be far stronger to try and repel us then for having the respite from our attention. A show of prolonged strength will have us sniffing around elsewhere.

So, we move on to the various manipulative techniques and how you can escape from them

# Intimidation

The purpose of intimidation is to generate fear. I will also do this to try and confuse you by using subtle threats of intimidation, which have you wondering whether they are real or not, and whether they will actually be acted on. This is done on purpose as you are then worried by them but also concerned not to cause a fuss and involve other people for fear of being seen to be over-reacting. Remember, I will of course suggest to third parties that you are imagining things and touched with a dose of 'the crazy'. Intimidation is the little brother to Anger in terms of exerting a method of control.

In order to deal with intimidation, remember that you are not over-reacting nor are you imagining things. I want you to believe that to be the case in order for my manipulation to have its effect on you. If you perceive I am intimidating you, then I am. You should record the act, making a brief note in order to use at a later date for the purpose of evidence should you need to

1. Convince others of my intimidating conduct. I might have got in first with other people but your diarised and written record will trump my oral recollection; and
2. You may need it as supporting evidence if it is necessary for you to escalate matters using formal means through the courts to protect

yourself or for example reporting the behaviour to a superior in a work context.

Do not make the mistake of showing me this documentary record in the hope of proving to me that I have been doing what you say I have been doing so I may recognise that and that I might change. That is not going to happen. All you have done is show me the evidence that I will then destroy and it will aggravate me resulting in a worsening of my behaviour towards you. Keep the record somewhere away from home (work is useful) or at a trusted friend or relatives. Make sure you update it. Do not be tempted to shy away from recording every act. They soon mount up and will prove very helpful. You may think others will regard it as trivial but does it feel trivial to you to be intimidated? There's your reason for doing it. Whilst we are touching on documenting behaviour you carry a camera and a video camera with you more or less all the time by virtue of your mobile phone. Use it to record my behaviour and then send the photo or footage to an email account you know I cannot access and from that send it another e-mail account (I may access your phone and see where the first email has been sent to). You should document and record throughout. There is never anything to be gained by showing this material to me as I will try to deny it (even though it speaks for itself) suggest you have obtained it out of context or even doctored it. I will not acknowledge the reality of what it shows as it does not accord with my reality. You will need these documented examples to remind yourself what you are escaping from, that you are not going mad when I gas light you and ultimately in support of more formal sanctions you may need to seek should the need arise. For the sake of brevity, I shall not mention this with each technique but always ensure you have a record of what has happened.

You need to remove yourself from the scope of the intimidating conduct so leave the room or the building where it is taking place. I am unlikely to escalate the conduct when you leave, as initially you will wrong foot me and I will be left wondering why you have done this, rather than stay and challenge me like you usually do. We are actually predictable creatures and we expect people to be similar. Often you act in the same fashion because our behaviour has been designed to achieve this and you have been conditioned to act in this way. By breaking the repetition of your behaviour it will leave us wrong footed and gives you an advantage.

Do not regard the intimidation as minor. It is not. It is a form of insidious control. By not reacting to it (either by complying or challenging) you are denying me a reaction and therefore I will soon stop. I may shift to other techniques (see below on how to look to nullify them) but by denying me any kind of reaction I will not waste any further energy on trying to intimidate you on this occasion.

Unfortunately for you I am not very good at learning lessons straight away so I will deploy intimidation again in the future, but you know how to deal with it. Calmly leave the situation and distance yourself from it. This immediately stops you having to be subjected to it so you feel better. The lack of reaction from you nullifies its potency so I will stop. You can make a note as part of your greater design for extricating yourself from me or managing my behaviour. If every time I try to intimidate you, you respond in this fashion, you will beat my attempt at manipulation on each occasion.

# Provocation

Healthy people in essence go through a four-stage process when making a decision. Firstly, they see the situation in front of them. Then they will assess the situation to ascertain precisely what is happening. Next they will identify the courses of action available to them before finally making a decision as to what they will do. I do not ordinarily engage in this process. I see a situation and then act or react. I am programmed to be this way because my responses are invariably based on certain triggers. I am like a vending machine; press a button and something happens without any need for consideration or assessment.

We expect you to behave in a similar fashion and therefore expect you to always react to what we do rather than carefully processing the behaviour. We do this by relying on a mechanism that means you bypass stages two and three. This mechanism is the fight or flight mode. When you are faced with certain stresses you will rely on deep-seated, rather than reasoned responses. I want that to happen, so that you will just react. One way of achieving this is to put you under pressure by provoking you. This may take the form of saying unpleasant things to you, flirting with other people to make you feel jealous, praising other friends to draw a reaction from you and so on. The purpose of this provocation is to engage your deep-seated immediate response rather than you considering the situation in a detached and calculated manner. This way we can make you do things, which you will come to regret as you acted very much in the heat of the moment.

We love getting a reaction from you and applying provocation is a prime way of doing so and we know it is geared up psychologically to create a reaction. You are best disabling this method of manipulation as follows: -

1. Be able to recognise provocation in its various forms. You will over time be aware of the more regular methods I might use (e.g. flirting with the opposite sex or name calling)

2. Is the matter being discussed something where a sensible resolution could be reached? If you do not fall into the trap of taking the bait, are you able to address the issue. You may be surprised that if you sidestep the provocation, you catch me unawares (I am focussed on provoking you and expect you to do that – after all you always have done in the past) and this can lead to an unexpected outcome whereby the matter being debated is resolved. Often it will not, so you need to determine, again by steering clear of provocation if this is a discussion that can achieve success or whether you are better maintaining a wide berth in its entirety. You will be surprised at just how much you actually know about me to work out which conversations can take place and which ones cannot.

3. Never engage in trying to appeal to a sense of reason or logic when I am seeking to provoke. I do not want to do that so I do not want you

to do that. I will just keep trying to provoke you until through frustration you will react and thus I will succeed. I also remember how long it takes to keep plugging away until you do react and therefore if you engage me I will continue until I get that result. Again, if you can nullify the provocation you may then engage in a sensible conversation. It is like defusing the bomb before you can remove it from the premises. Nullify the provocation and then determine where the conversation can go to next – constructive discussion or a walk away.

4. You must turn the other cheek. Maintain calm and do not rise to the bait. I will realise that my provocation is not working and therefore I will disengage. I will see no value in continuing to try and elicit a reaction from you.

5. Do not retaliate by trying to provoke me or trading insults. I want a fight. This provides me with fuel.

6. If I am trying to provoke you by means of a false allegation, issue a rebuttal once. I will not accept it but you will have laid down a marker for your own peace of mind. You know you have told the truth to me, it is my problem that I have not accepted it. This is also helpful to assist you in engaging the assistance of others if you are looking to address a particular issue, which is the subject of the provocation. You are able to demonstrate you have acted reasonably without unnecessarily entering into a fight.

# Anger

In order to deal with my anger, you need to understand what is going through my mind when I am angry. I am enraged because I regard you as being at fault. Invariably you will not be but that does not matter. You have upset me; most likely by criticising me (real or imagined) this means that all I can hear is the roar of the flames. I do not hear anything you are saying, I cannot see what you are showing me in a document or in a video recording. A lot of the time you will be trying to engage with me to show that you are correct and that I am not. My mind does not work like that. I am right all the time (although this is not the same thing as being correct). I regard you as inferior to me and therefore you are always wrong or at fault. This angers me. There is nothing you can do to make me change my mind. This is my default setting and is ingrained inside of me. Never attempt to show I am wrong. This is infuriating but all you will do is stoke the anger further, which is likely to be dangerous for you and your property. You are not able to make me see the error of my behaviour so you may as well save your energy and instead channel it into ensuring that the effect of my fierce wrath on you is minimised as far as you possibly can.

If the anger is manifested by physical violence towards you or property you must do the following: -

1. Ensure dependents are safe;

2. Get away from the source of the violence; and

## 3. Call the police

There is little point hoping to placate a narcissist once he or she is engaged in a rage, which is causing damage to person or property. However great you feel the temptation to try and placate them or soothe them, it will not work. We cannot hear you. We just see you in front of us and this infuriates us all the more. Your weakness in the face of our assault reinforces your inferiority and riles us as we are reminded that we are with you and we hate ourselves for being with you. Our rage is blind, furious and incandescent. We lash out at anything and anyone around us. It is a toddler tantrum on a huge and dangerous scale.

By remaining in our line of sight you are provoking us all the more. Your safety and that of children, relatives and pets is what you should be concentrating on. Remove yourself and others to neighbours, another relative or even getting in the car and driving around until you can summon help. More often than not we will not follow you (although this is not always the case) but we are so engrossed in our rage that we fail to notice something unless it is front of us. If you stay and try and talk to us, you are immediately in the line of fire and you will be attacked. This is because you have increased our rage by being there and you are there to be attacked. By leaving us to it, there is more chance of our rage burning out and we will direct it at inanimate objects around us. It is not pleasant knowing your house is being smashed up but that is better than you or your children being injured. Wait for the police to handle the situation.

If the anger is shouting and insults, you should also consider removing yourself from the situation for the reasons outlined above and the very fact that it is unpleasant to be subjected to such verbal abuse. There is however less of a need to depart and especially if there are practical considerations (children asleep or an infirm relative) you may prefer to utilise an alternative technique to manage this rage.

Do not engage in aggression yourself. This will escalate our rage and could possibly push us towards physical violence when none has been exhibited before or so far. By acting aggressively, you are criticising us and therefore pouring more fuel on the fire. You are also seen to be challenging our superiority, which will keep the rage burning.

Don't continue the conversation. We are not hearing anything you are saying to us. You may be able to move to another room and leave us to what in effect is a tantrum.

Aim to remain calm. This may be difficult as your natural reaction may be to fight back, especially if the rage is accompanied by ridiculous allegations, but by keeping calm and showing no reaction you will be cutting off our fuel. We will see that we are not getting any reaction from you and that is the purpose of rage, to provoke a response in you. Once this fails, we realise it is pointless expending any further energy and we will stop. The rage burns itself out. It may take considerable discipline to maintain calm and remain collected but you will reap the dividends in bringing the rage to a conclusion far more quickly. Think about how a toddler stops when nobody is paying any attention to the tantrum. The similar principle applies here. Eventually we will probably walk off and sit and sulk somewhere. Leave us to it. You have stopped the rage.

Do not feel the need to try and fix the situation. This is our rage, not yours. You have caused it in our warped minds but in reality you have not. You should not feel any responsibility or obligation for our anger and rage. It is not your creation and therefore you have no need to try and address its cause. Do not feel guilty or blame yourself in any way. The whole reason we have engaged in anger and rage is down to the way we look at the world and the way we are wired. It is not your fault.

# Gas lighting

Gas lighting is a particularly insidious method of controlling you. I will present to you a completely convincing front whereby I could not possibly be wrong even though your perception of the situation suggests that I am. I behave with an overwhelming sense of conviction so that you will question yourself and your own judgement.

The key with addressing gas lighting is to recognise it is happening at the earliest juncture to avoid its terrible impact from gaining a hold. Once it has, no matter how hard you try, you will struggle to imprint your reality on the situation and will invariably acquiesce to what I am saying as being the truth of the situation, even though it is a fabrication.

1. I am not going to accept your version of events, your recall or your recollection. I am convinced that I am right, as that is why I am engaging in gas lighting. If you try to convince me to the contrary, you are giving me attention and engaging in my warped creation. It will often please me to see you trying to challenge me as this is giving me attention. I know that you will not succeed and all you are doing is feeding me and exhausting and frustrating yourself.

2. Instead, reinforce the fact that you are correct. If you have got into the habit of recording certain key events and decisions (you may be doing this to counter intimidation) then you have a written record. Again, do not produce this to me in order to try and convince me

that you are right because look, here it is written down. I will just accuse you of having written it down that instant, or if you did it earlier you have misremembered. Use the recording to reinforce in your own mind that you are correct and preserve your correct perception of reality so you do not start to slide into the false reality I have created.

3. I am especially skilled at manipulating arguments and running rings around you in an argument. Keep at the forefront of your mind that just because I am doing this does not mean that my arguments are valid. I will try and blind you into submission with dazzling but ultimately ill-conceived arguments. You must not think I am right just because I appear to be winning the argument through conniving behaviour.

4. Do not be afraid to rely on your supporters to validate your position. I will denigrate them as well and suggest they are not to be relied on. You need not tell me that they support you, as I will not accept this. You should use this to reinforce your own position and utilise it as security. It will also assist your frame of mind to be able to share what is happening to you.

5. Do not blame yourself for the way I am behaving and do not think you can fix it. That is impossible and you will only be exposing yourself to my machinations again if you do.

6. Focus on sensible and practical thoughts about you. I want you to see the world as I create it. You must fight against that and to do this you need to keep yourself firmly in the real world. If you allow

yourself to think about my behaviour, you will get sucked back into my false reality.

# Love Bombing

My massive attention overload, charm offensive, verbal seduction and flattery along with excessive communication, gift giving and other worldly enchantment all make up love bombing. I am rather pleased that people actually refer to it as love bombing as that makes it sound like a pleasant experience. I know that when it is happening it certainly feels wonderful for you but as you will now be aware it has a much more sinister objective. One thing you would do well at the outset is to change the label. It is grooming. That description signals danger and so it should. This grooming is actually the major defence you should hone. If you see through this seduction and do not fall for it, then you will avoid all of the other manipulative techniques that I utilise. Grooming is the bridge into my citadel of anguish and regret. You need to ensure you do not cross it and instead burn it down so there is never any temptation to go and walk over that bridge. How might you go about beating my grooming, given the heightened level of charm and seduction that accompanies it?

1. Those combatting fraud live by the adage of "if it seems too good to be true, it usually is." Adopt that mantra at the outset of a relationship. There is nothing wrong with someone sending you amorous texts but not fifty a day. Sending flowers is romantic but does not have to be a weekly occurrence. Recognise the substance of a compliment. If someone praises your hairstyle after you have been

to the hairdresser, then that makes sense. If they repeatedly talk about how athletic, honed and appealing your body is when it isn't, you know the compliment is not realistic. Pay special attention to outlandish declarations of love and commitment such as: -

"You are my soul mate"

"I will die if we aren't together"

"I have never loved anyone like I love you."

"I love you and I always have"

Look out for some choice examples in the seduction stage of my book **Evil** as well. Remember those phrases and keep them as watchword to your heart. Again, somebody saying some of these phrases makes sense after several months of spending time together, not after two dates. If you find yourself vaguely embarrassed by the comment or you regard it as toe curling, trust your instincts. You are being flattered to deceive.

2. Beware of my kind and me saying that we have some kind of special connection very early on in the relationship. How on earth can we have that if we have only recently met? Do not fall for explanations such as "we have known each other a long time". Yes, we may have but that was as colleagues or people who passed in the street. It was not on an intimate basis. We love to make you feel special and will

refer to this spiritual connection that we have or an intense sexual bonding (even though all we have ever done is kiss so far).

3. If I seem to know a lot about you, be wary. How could I possibly know all that unless I have been stalking you? Normally we find out about one another through spending time together and conversing. If I seem to have an encyclopaedic knowledge about your likes and dislikes, I have been heavily researching you already. That is not healthy.

4. If I appear to be sharing a lot of secrets with you, you should be vigilant about this as well. I do this to make you my co-conspirator and draw you into my web of deceit. I am doing it to make you feel special and also in the hope that you will yield secrets to me which I can then use to threaten you at a later stage. Would you tell someone you had only met once before your most intimate secrets? No you would not. So why am I?

5. Pay careful attention to how I talk about other people in my life. Am I dismissive about family? Do I have few long-standing friends? Chances are these people have already worked me out and therefore I have discarded them. Not everyone is Waltonesque with their family or has a stable of longstanding friends but it is certainly an indicator.

6. How do I refer to my exes? If it is with bitterness and labelling them as nasty and crazy, your narcometer should be flashing at this point. We all have reasons to dislike our exes – we either got rid of them or they got rid of us – but the tone, extent and manner by which we

refer to them should not be malevolent or hateful. If it is, there is a clear warning for you.

7. When we first meet do I cover a lot of topics with you? If so be wary of this especially if I seem to change opinions about certain things or like somethings, which are diametrically opposed. I am working my way through a checklist of items by which I intend to ascertain which you like and which you do not, so I can then agree with you as part of my mirroring technique but also to create a false bond between us.

8. Trust your gut instinct. Would you say and do the things that I do so soon? Yes, we all approach relationships differently, but a healthy approach is one of cautious interest as we find out about one another. If it is too fast, too wonderful and too fantastic, chances are it is false.

9. Are our early conversations all about you and little about me? Whilst we narcissists are well known for wanting to direct everything back to ourselves, we will share the limelight or even pass it up at first for the greater gain. If you are learning very little about me (other than I agree with what you like and dislike) there is a reason for this. I have something to hide. I move in the shadows.

10. If you are finding my behaviour too overpowering in the early stages distance yourself. I want to engulf you and my desire to do this overrides any sense of proportionate behaviour on my part. I also do not recognise normal boundaries (see Boundary Violation below).

11. Be cautious of excessive gestures such as expensive gifts and trips. It feels exhilarating to receive them but again they are designed to sweep you off your feet and get you off your guard.

12. Talk to your trusted friends about what is happening. You should share these developments with friends. Pay attention to what they may say in response. I won't have had chance yet to condition these people to like me or even recruit them as my lieutenants. I am unlikely to denigrate them too much for fear of alarming you. This is a narrow window of opportunity for you to receive some independent advice about how it really looks from someone not caught up in my maelstrom.

13. Maintain vigilance for discrepancies. I am prone to bragging about my achievements and boasting about matters such as job, money and popularity. Check these assertions against information from third parties to establish whether what I have said is true. Why not undertake a credit check against me to establish if my declarations of solvency are true?

14. Observe how I react to you having friends of the opposite sex. I am not able to tolerate you showing an interest in other people, especially those of the opposite sex and I will engage in disparaging behaviour about those people or do something which means you have to divert your attention to me. Invariably this behaviour will be childish in nature, such as purposefully spilling a drink or just happening to break something so it requires your attention and takes it away from your friend.

# Reflection

When I reflect, I am deflecting from my own odious behaviours and removing accountability for them. I am also accusing you of doing what I am guilty of to achieve this removal of responsibility and to also demean you. I am blaming you for what I have done. I may say things such as

"You made me do it because you don't love me."

"This is your fault. You made this happen."

"You never help me do the household chores do you?"

Usually the projection is based on a fabrication. I need to do this in order to effect the projection but it also serves a purpose by way of provoking you. Bear in mind the points made above in that regard. In dealing with my projection you are best served as follows: -

1. Remain calm and do not engage in an argument with me. I want you to react. If you try and accuse me of reflection my rage will increase.

2. Do not accept any blame for what I am projecting onto you. Keep reminding yourself that the problem is mine. It is not your problem. You should not tell me that the problem is mine, as this will provoke me. However, if you keep telling yourself that it is not your problem, this will assist your state of mind.

3. State the truth of the matter and do so on one occasion only. You have laid down your marker. I will not accept it but you know you have told the truth and this will help you. Remember, these techniques are not designed to help you change me (that is impossible) it is about enabling you to manage the effect of my behaviour on you. By calmly stating the truth on one occasion you

will feel validated. If need be, this might also be witnessed in some way (a third party or filmed) and thus you know you have given the truth to me. I chose to ignore it.

4. Do not absorb the blame that I am reflecting onto you. All you are doing is enabling me and eroding your own self-esteem. Keep in mind that my position is not based on facts (no matter how persuasive I may sound and how convinced I am in the legitimacy of my argument). I am blaming you to make me feel better and this happens to make you feel worse. It is nothing to do with the truth. I also am oblivious, during this episode of reflection, that my behaviour is not actually solving the real problem. Thus it is impossible for you to engage me in a meaningful fashion.

5. Do not believe that I am reflecting blame on to you from a logical standpoint. I am not.

6. Do not alter your behaviour because of my reflected blame. It is my problem. It is not your problem. If you start making changes based on my reflection, I will note this and do it all the more. You will erode your sense of self based on a false premise.

7. Although it is an attack against you, my primary purpose is to try and make me feel better about myself. I am trying to cast off the faults I am guilty of. If you think of it in this manner, it will feel less of a personal attack. You will see my reflection for what it really is. It is about me, not about you.

8. Politely end the conversation and move away. By failing to engage in an argument arising from my reflecting you are reducing the fuel I can garner from the situation and this will often leave me unable to pursue the reflection.

# Guilt

I use guilt as a less intense method of control. On my part, it does not take a lot of effort to utilise this technique. One of the more difficult parts about dealing with guilt is actually recognising that it is being used against you. I usually do it by making a remark that I know will cause you to feel guilty, even though the comment may be wrapped up in an apparent compliment.

Typical remarks take the following form: -

"If you really loved me you would do it."

"I know how much you love me and that is why I know you will do this for me."

"All my friends say you are being unfair by not agreeing to let me go with them on a short golfing trip."

"I work hard to provide for you and the family and you never let me have time to myself."

"If you leave I will kill myself."

"I know how caring you are and that's why I know you will help me."

"Do you know how much you hurt me when you look at someone else?"

"What would your parents/best friend/ vicar/ boss think of your behaviour?"

"If you go home now, I will be left in the bar on my own."

"You are better than me at looking after the children, so that's why I should go out really isn't it?"

"If you don't work late how will you ever secure that promotion?"

"After everything I do for you and you won't do this one small thing for me?"

"Come on, everyone does this. You don't want me having to tell people that you are frigid and prudish do you?"


1.      Always resist giving in to my attempt to make you feel guilty. If you do, I will keep doing it because I know that it is effective. If I know I can make you feel guilty and thus control you, I will keep engaging in the behaviour and it will become worse as I demand more and push you further to comply.

2.      Not only will your resistance prevent the situation from worsening it has a very good chance of preventing me using the technique again or at least often. It is often hard to deal with my use of guilt. Often you do not realise I am doing it and if you do, you feel bad and want to stop feeling bad so you give in. That is a typical empathic reaction and why you have been chosen. I know that you like to enable people. I know that you like to facilitate and I also know that you dislike the feeling of having upset someone or let him or her down. My use of guilt plays on all these healthy traits of yours. You need to develop a rigidity of character to recognise guilt is being used and moreover to stand up to it. It is hard but the reward

will be significant for you. Why is that so? As with many of my techniques, I prefer to use the least amount of energy and secure the maximum return by way of control and fuel from you. Thus, if you refuse to give in to my guilt trips then you are adopting a position, which will cause me to expend more energy. I am then likely to stop doing it. By showing me resistance I will usually shrug and see it does not work and give up trying. I am not willing to use my precious resources when the likelihood of success is low. Remember, I love to win. I am a creature of economy (although you already knew that didn't you seeing as you always end up paying for dinner).

2.      The guilt is not about anything you have done wrong. Do not fall into the trap of analysing your own behaviour in order to agree with and appease me. As is often the case, it is my problem. It is not your problem.

3.      Be alert to situations where I am seeking to control you by feeling guilty. Read about such manipulative behaviours. As with many of my tactics, you do not actually realise what I am doing until it is too late. You need to ensure that you are educated about the way I apply guilt in our relationship, whether it is an intimate one or a professional or social one. This is where gut instinct proves to be valuable. If you feel the slightest degree of discomfort at what I am saying, even if what you are actually hearing is complimentary, then be aware I am utilising guilt. By recognising when I am applying this technique you will then be far abler to negate it.

4.    Establish where your boundaries are. You may not have a difficulty in being the more giving in the relationship. If you are comfortable with that, that is not an issue. It is knowing when your boundaries are being crossed so that you feel uncomfortable.

5.    Understand that I am only concerned about getting what I want. Any promises I may attach to the utilisation of guilt will be empty ones.

# Lieutenants

I always keep a coterie of loyal admirers. As I have explained in **Manipulated** these are drawn from a variety of places with the purpose of ensuring that I obtain control and fuel through their willing assistance. My lieutenants (some call them flying monkeys) are there to carry out by proxy all of my various forms of manipulation. They are doubly dangerous. Firstly, they allow me to enhance my effect since many hands undertaking my malign activities will increase their impact. Secondly, you may work out what I am doing but be oblivious to a proxy continuing my work on my behalf. You may think you can counter me but you have not calculated for me having henchmen to continue my dirty work.

One of the most important things that my Lieutenants do is to ensure that you are regarded as the troublemaker. Since I have a number of people supporting my position, it will automatically erode yours. With repetition, you will start to believe it yourself.

1. The starting point is to recognise who those Lieutenants are. I expand on this in **Manipulated** but you need to be aware of those who blindly follow me, always accept what I say without question, always disagree with you and cannot be persuaded despite convincing evidence being placed before them. It is often very difficult to spot these people. Some will be drawn from long-standing friends of mine (I do have a few); others will be subordinates at work and perhaps a neighbour. I

have even used therapists in this way. I have asked them to speak to a partner about her non-existent addiction issues. Pay close attention to my friends of the opposite sex. I usually always seduce them so if I have not done so there must be some other reason for me keeping them close to me. Be aware that I will definitely seek to recruit Lieutenants from your family and friends. These are the most powerful Lieutenants that I can find and those, which cause the greatest damage to you. Once you know what I am, you then need to pick out my Lieutenants. My kind and me always have them. We need them to admire and fawn over us and we need them to carry out our machinations for us too. Identification of these individuals is key for you.

2. Cultivate a healthy scepticism. Just because somebody has said something it does not mean that it is true. I know this flies in the face of what you stand for. You tell the truth and therefore you expect other people to do so as well. You act with honesty and thus believe other people should. However, since you have worked out either through your own observation or the assistance of your reading or the advice of others, that I am a pathological liar, it follows that those associated with me may well be tainted by the same affliction. Thus, you need to train yourself to question and seek corroboration about anything someone associated with me may say. By adopting this approach, you will not stop my Lieutenants from telling lies (they are far too conditioned to my influence to do this) but you will be able to ameliorate their effect on you.

3. Seek verification of what you are told. Remember, the Lieutenants are my conduits and accordingly you need to seek independent verification as to what they are saying is true.

4. Pay particular regard to anybody who has links to me who holds a position of authority. I aim to recruit these individuals as people are naturally conditioned to believe, respect and obey authority (of course, ironically, I am not). If you know that I have a connection to someone such as a police officer, council official, teacher and the like, you must be wary of their behaviour towards you also.

5. Do not try and persuade my Lieutenants that you are right and they are wrong. I choose people who have a firm belief that they are right and they will react unfavourably to any criticism from you. You will also be wasting your time. They have already been brainwashed by me to see you as the difficult one, the abusive one and the crazy one. Anything you do which contradicts that established view will only serve to reinforce their established view of you.

6. Do not argue with my lieutenants. They will see this as reinforcement of the established view. They will also feed this back to me. This is a useful form of secondary fuel for me. It also provides me with material to attack you.

"Why have you been going behind my back and speaking to my friends about me?"

"Why have you been pestering my friends?"

"Why have you been talking about our problems to other people. That's our business. Are you trying to embarrass me and make me look stupid?"

7.  Do not ask them whose side are you on? They are on my side. Always. This criticism of them will only result in them taking an even dimmer view of you. They may be your family members but what use are they to you, if they have taken my side in these matters? Do not expect them to support you just because you are related or because you became friends with them first. My charm and manipulation has worked on them as well. They believe I am wonderful and they believe you are the problem. They will not want to look foolish by siding with "the troublemaker" so don't waste your energy.

8.  You have no need to take my Lieutenants seriously. They are just an extension of me and will do my bidding and carry out my work. It is not their true opinion of you but rather one they have been in effect instructed to have by me.

9.  Once you have established who these Lieutenants are you will know not to pass them information, which will then be passed on to me. You can block them from social media so their capability to be a messenger for me is much reduced. They lack the drive and sophistication to try and overcome any obstacles you may put in place for them. They will not apply themselves in a driven manner, unlike me. Instead, they will just become negated. When I ask them what you have been doing, they will explain that they do not know as they have been blocked on

Twitter and Facebook, but they will do nothing more to try and surmount that problem. They are extensions of me but they are not me. They lack my ingenuity and power. Accordingly, once you know who they are, you are able to neutralise their effect rather quickly and effectively.

# Circular Conversations

This method of manipulation is tiring, frustrating and designed to wear you down. It seizes on your desire to bring a conversation to a close and reach a resolution. This is linked to your deep-seated desire to have us see the error of our ways and somehow be fixed. If you can conclude the discussion you feel that you have made some headway and progress. You might have even been able to cause me to reconsider my position. Of course this does not happen and this is why you find it especially frustrating. We are experts at going round and round because we ignore logic, as we believe we are always right in what we are saying. This enables us to cast aside anything sensible and logical that you may say and allows us to rely on a nonsensical comment as if it was a wise judgement.

One way that we do this is to make statements that are designed to provide an emotional response from you, rather than making a factual statement. You will be able to identify these statements as we will often use 'always' and 'never' in order to distort grossly the facts and then cause you to want to argue further with us to try and demonstrate how the statement we just made is wholly incorrect.

"You never show me any affection."

"You are always stopping me from doing what I want."

On the face of it these are clearly ridiculous statements. (In fact it is more likely that you should be saying these comments to me, but that's another matter) and thus hearing me say them will cause you to become irritated and angry and thus provide us with an emotional reaction. We will use these words often in the context of a circular argument.

You need to keep the following in mind when you are dealing with the deployment of a Circular Argument.

1. Just because I am saying something with conviction and supposed authority does not mean that it is correct. Just because I keep repeating it will not add to the force of the argument. You knew it was wrong the first time I said it. Why should you change from that position if I repeat it? That is what I am trying to do though. I want you to accept what I am saying by reason of being worn down through the circular nature of the conversation. I subscribe to the view that if I say it loud and often enough you will accept what I am saying. I win arguments by intimidation, not through the application of logic.

2. Do not lose your temper when I am taking you around in circles. Yes, it is frustrating as this is what this tactic is designed for. I want you

to explode in frustration as this gives me the emotional reaction that I am seeking.

3.  Do not repeat yourself. You have said it once. There is no need to repeat what you have said. I am not listening to you anyway. I do not hear your words. I just sense an emotional response from you, which is what I want. I just hear what I am saying. You will only end up frustrated.

4.  Do not seek refuge in aggressive gestures to convey how frustrated you are instead of shouting or being insulting. This is still a reaction and this is what I want. If you storm off, slam a door or throw something, I have succeeded.

5.  Be able to recognise the pattern. Identify that the conversation is going nowhere. I am adept at masking this at times and I am just toying with you, taking you round and round. You need to spot what I am doing and then you can address it.

6.  Don't spend your time talking about what I am saying. If you say to me,

"You are talking rubbish"

"You are being aggressive"

"You are lying"

This will only provoke me. Trying to gain the upper hand by making such comments may break the circular nature of the discussion but it will only result in me becoming enraged and lashing out at you.

7.  Do not expect to reach an outcome. You expect this with normal healthy people but do keep in mind that even those conversations can result in a lack of agreement. Just because I am especially obstinate and difficult, it does not mean that our conversations cannot naturally reach a position of non-agreement.

8.  If you have already answered one of my questions do not waste your time answering it again. You have given your response. If I cannot deal with your response, then that is my issue. It is not yours.

9.  Feel free to state how you are feeling. This gives you a sense of relief and validation. I will try and contradict you but how can I? They are your feelings, not mine. Keep that in your mind, you do not need to tell me that. Revel in keeping that useful knowledge to yourself and enjoy being able to express your feelings knowing they cannot be challenged. The conversation may not get anywhere but you will feel less frustrated because you have been able to say how you feel. This will also irritate me because I do not want to know how you feel, I am content to see how you feel because this is what I aim for. I also want you to listen to how I feel and if you are talking about your feelings then this results in my control being eroded. If you are now aware that you are eroding my control, this will empower you and thus what

seemed to be a fruitless conversation will actually result in a form of positive outcome for you.

10.      End the conversation if need be. Explain you need a break and walk away. Do it politely and calmly. We are seeking an emotional reaction from you. A levelheaded one has no benefit for us and results in us being wrong-footed. Often we will just slink away, slightly confused by your reaction, leaving you alone.

# Denial

This is another technique from the stable of frustration. We deploy it when we are on the back foot. We are not able to gain any leverage to attack you. You have successfully avoided providing us with any fuel as you approach us in a calm manner and level an accusation against us. Reflecting or Projection isn't serving any purpose and therefore we will rely on Denial. We do this to maintain our asserted superiority. We are denying you the ability and right to judge us. We also hope that if we deny it enough times you will become frustrated and either give up (thus freeing us from being backed into a corner and feeling very uncomfortable as we have ceded control to you) or you lose your temper or cry (thus giving us an emotional reaction and accordingly fuel). So, what ought you to do when faced with repeated denial?

1.      Understand that we believe our version of reality to be the correct version. We do not see the world in the way that you and others do. We may look at the same things but we see them very differently. Grasping this can be difficult and exasperating, but once you have done so, it will confer a large advantage to you. To put it bluntly, you and everyone else may see a fireplace but to us it is a television and no matter how much your describe the features of a fireplace, all we will hear is you contradicting and criticising us, not what you are actually explaining in a logical fashion. This may take some time for you to comprehend. Once

you have done so however, it will mean you realise that there is little you can do to alter it. It will also enable you to realise why it is that we are so fastidious in our denials. We truly believe what we are saying is correct. It may not add up in the normal world, but I do not reside there.

2.     Grasping the above concept is very important. As an empathic individual you are programmed to want to fix us. You believe that we will suddenly see the light if you are just able to make us listen, put the argument a different way or show us something different. This is a tiring and fruitless task on your part. You will not achieve any success and all you will do is expend a huge amount of effort getting nowhere. It is understandable because that is the way you are, but you need to understand that your usual kind and caring approach will not work in halting our denials.

3.     Since I do not operate in your reality, your norms and the usual conversational conventions all go out of the window. You can tell me the cat is white and I will swear that it is black. That is because in my world it is black. The sooner you realise this, the easier your life will become.

4.     Don't assume I am aware of how much of a contrarian I am being. Often I am issuing denials because they assist me in trying to recover control and get me out of the corner. I know you are right but I am forbidden from admitting it as this causes me to lose. I hate losing. Other times, I have no idea that I am wrong because in my altered reality I am correct. Either way, you must understand that I am not going to concede

and therefore you can save yourself the banging your head against a brick wall routine.

5. Do not fall into the trap of agreeing with my denial just to relieve the frustration. You know you are correct but keep that within yourself. I am as I am. Accept that and realise we have to disagree. Even though in the normal world you are correct, you are not going to win the argument with me. I know that is difficult to swallow, as you know I am intelligent and therefore surely I must accept the truth of what you are saying? I am disordered. I either will not or cannot accept what you say. I must deny. The result is always the same. Accept it and move on.

6. Just because I maintain the denial does not mean that you are wrong. Nor must you think that my denial should define you. There is nothing to be served in troubling yourself about how my denial makes you look.

7. Turn to those friends and supporters on whom you can rely for validation that your position is correct. You need not deal with my denial alone.

8. If the allegation that you are making is of a serious nature and I continue to issue denials, document and/or film the exchange in case you need to rely on it. Naturally this should only be reserved for the serious issues and not a situation where I deny eating the last biscuit in the jar!

9. Do not turn to my Lieutenants to support you or to try and recruit them to persuade me that my denial is incorrect. You will never persuade

me for the reasons outlined above and my Lieutenants are of no use to you either.

10.    Maintain calm. Dealing with someone who appears to be denying the obvious is at the hair-pulling end of the scale of frustration but you always need to keep in mind that any kind of emotional reaction from you plays straight into our hands. Remaining calm and in control eats away at us and asserts your strength, something we do not want to witness.

## Attrition

Attrition or by its more widely recognised name, bullying, is a blunt instrument of coercion. For my part, as a sophisticated abuser, I do not like to rely on it. I find it rather uncouth and obvious. It is certainly effective as it will have the person on the receiving end feeling weak and frightened and therefore it is a fast method of grabbing control. I prefer to utilise subtler and insidious methods. These avoid detection by you and by others. Bullying you by wearing you down lacks subtlety and can often prove to be the final straw for many people, resulting in them taking decisive action to escape our clutches.

Should a target do this, we will have to expend greater levels of energy to pursue them and extract fuel from them. There is also the risk that in bullying them in such a blunt manner, they have been able to collect useful evidence, which the authorities will pay heed to and act on to our detriment. All of these points result in it being rarely used by me, but I include it as many of my brethren do utilise it.

From my perspective the fundamental reason why I dislike it as it is evidence of losing control. I do not like to feel my grip on you is slipping. By engaging in bullying, I am utilising last resort tactics and that is of concern to me. I must have control at all times and by using bullying I am seeking to assert control again quickly and in a blunt manner. Bullying may take a verbal, emotional or physical form and is designed to grind you down so you will do, as I want. The physical bullying is obvious; the assault on an individual to ensure they act as we want by reason of the fear of the infliction of pain. Verbal bullying will be shouting, the systematic and repeated hurling of insults, often done in a rage. There is little that is covert or insidious about this technique. Instead it is obvious and demeaning. I may utilise it when I feel frustrated that other methods of manipulation are not working. It is a sudden and nasty explosion of coercion.

It tends to rear its head when you have exhibited defiance. My usual subtle methods of manipulation may not be delivering and instead you have drawn some strength from somewhere and accordingly you are beginning to defy me and stand up to me. I will not tolerate any challenge to my method of control. I must reassert it and quickly. In those circumstances I turn to bullying you over and over to grind you down. How ought you tackle this form of manipulation when it appears?

1.     If you fear for your person, or that of another, immediately remove yourself from the scene and call the police. Ensure others in your care are safe as well. You cannot challenge those of my kind who erupt into physical violence. Those who are trained to combat violence and those who have the force of the law behind them must do this. Get out and call them out.

2.     Do not think that if the bullying is not physical that its effect on you is in any way diminished. In many respects verbal abuse and emotional bullying is worse. You are less likely to be believed. Do not think somehow that you have to deal with it. You do not have to do. If possible, remove yourself from the source of the bullying behaviour. Go to a friend's house or some other supporter so you are removed from the poisonous behaviour.

3.     Do not tolerate bullying. It will not go away. If we see it work, like with any of our manipulative techniques, we will keep using it. You must act to end it and do so promptly.

4.     Do not argue or retaliate. This is what we want. We want an emotional reaction from you. This gives us fuel but it also gives us a basis for asserting you are the one at fault. If a third party arrives we want you to be argumentative, hysterical and foaming at the mouth. With the speed of a flicked switch, we will suddenly be the epitome of calm and charmed politeness. The upshot of this is that you will not be believed and you may even find yourself being taken away by the police.

5.     Record and/or document the behaviour should you feel it is necessary to escalate a procedure with regard to your safety.

6.     The most effective way of rendering our bullying impotent is to leave. We cannot bully an empty space. Sometimes this maybe as simple as ending an aggressive conversation in a firm manner. On another occasion it may mean leaving the room or even the property.

7.     Whilst unpleasant to deal with by understanding my perspective as to why bullying is being used, you should garner some hope and encouragement from it. I am losing control and using a band-aid method to try and re-assert it. As I have explained above, I rarely use it, but those who do may find their hold over you is about to end. Firstly, by using bullying you are now aware that the hold is slipping and this will strengthen you to persevere in your plans to escape. Secondly, since bullying is such an inelegant manipulative tool it leaves too much evidence. You are then able to use that evidence to turn opinion against me, validate your position and persuade people in authority of my wrongdoing. Thus, if you are experiencing bullying you must remove yourself from it and then press on in taking action against my kind and me to try and sever our hold over you.

Bullying is brutal but it signals the end is in sight and we are struggling to maintain our hold over you. Keep that at the forefront of your mind.

# Isolation

This is a highly effective technique of manipulating you. By removing your contacts and support networks you are left exposed to the full effect of how we wish to control you. You have nobody to turn to for help, you have nobody to validate what you see and feel and since you have nobody you become more determined to hold onto me, thus giving me free reign to control you and ruin your life. How do you tackle isolation?

1.     Identify it. My method of isolating you is extremely subtle and is always done under the pretence of doing the best thing for you. I will point out how certain friends say things about you so you do not want to spend time with them (this will coincide with me saying to your friends that you have said certain things about them or by me being generally obnoxious to them that they have no desire to be around us. As you will be aware from my earlier writings, I will be endeavouring to spend all of my time with you, so that you will not want anyone else and nobody else will want to be around us because of my behaviour. You won't notice or if you happen to do so, you will not care as I will be solidly Love Bombing you.) I will drive a wedge between you and family members, often picking up on small issues between you, which you will have mentioned to me as I pumped you for information in the seduction stage of our relationship. My carefully orchestrated campaign of whispers and smears (which will be visiting you of course in the fullness of time) will ensure you are neatly

isolated with a near surgical precision. You need to be aware that it is happening. Watch out keenly for the following: -

- Am I commenting adversely on people you would ordinarily spend time with?
- Am I persuading you to forgo your interests (watching sport, attending a club, doing an activity) under the guise of wanting to spend more time together?
- Do I book your weekend up in advance for you but pass it off as treating you?
- Am I ever present when you are on the telephone to your family and friends?
- Are you making excuses as to why you cannot attend events?
- Reflect on when you last met with friends, families, group members, team members and the like.

By monitoring this behaviour, you will realise far sooner that I am isolating you. Once you realise this is happening and you try to counter it be prepared for a major charm offensive from me. I will put you under significant pressure in order to maintain my mission of cutting you off from your support networks. I will apply different manipulative techniques (Guilt, Threatened Loss, Pity and Triangulation in particular) to ensure you become isolated. You must remain resolute. Once you realise what I am doing you can keep your networks in place. You need to see your friends regularly. They will validate your position on my other behaviours and also provide you with support. Friends and family will act as an indispensable buffer or safe-zone where you can at the very least obtain some respite from my machinations and at best rely on them for help and advice to negate my manipulation of you.

2.      If you have not been able to identify the isolation and therefore have failed to stop it before it has taken effect all is not lost. You must keep in mind that although you feel alone, you are not alone. You will be surprised how accommodating friends and family will be despite the manner in which you have not bothered with them for some time. Do not feel ashamed and embarrassed to approach them. I am relying on this as a device for keeping you apart from them. Overcome that sense and approach them. You need them. It is likely that having isolated you so effectively; I will have unleashed all my other methods of control against you. This will leave you feeling weak, exhausted and confused. This is when you need the assistance of people you can trust more than ever. I know this and I will strive to keep you apart from them and maintain your isolation. I will pour lies into your ears about how they do not want to see you. The reality is they often ring but I always answer your phone and get rid of them. I hide any cards they send to you so you think they have ignored your birthday and Christmas. Any gifts they might send are intercepted by me and sold, hidden or destroyed. Keeping you in isolation is one of the central planks of my manipulation of you and I will stop at nothing to achieve it and maintain it. You need to know you will be in for

a fight as you try to reconnect with the people I have pulled you away from, but you need to persevere.

3. I know you will find it very hard to break the silence and I am counting on that so you decide to remain isolated. Keep in mind there is only so much I can do to keep you away from people, especially with the advantages conveyed by technology. Keeping you incommunicado when you comply is easy; it is draining for me when you are active in trying to get in touch with people.

4. Wrong foot me. I will be mindful you will be trying to contact family, certain friends, colleagues and so on who I was aware of when we first met. I am trying to cover all exits. Look to engage with someone I might not know of - a therapist is often an excellent choice, or a spiritual leader. You need to identify someone who will understand your position, will not feed back to me that you have been in touch and someone who I will not be aware of. If you do this, you will be surprised at the effect it will have in giving you help and encouragement.

5. My method of isolation is not just about cutting you off from the people that matter to you. It is also about removing from you the things, which give you joy and instead replacing them with the joy, which I pretend to give you instead. You need to understand for my work on you to be effective and give me maximum control; I need you to become addicted and dependent on me. I want you living and breathing through me. At first I will tell you this and you will feel it is romantic. It is far more sinister. I want to be your life support machine and you cannot live

without me. I control the switch that determines whether you live or fade away. That is the ultimate control I want over you. To create that level of dependency I must wrench you away from people but also everything you enjoy. Thus I will change your taste in films, music, food, entertainment and so on. I will stop you doing those things so that ultimately you forget that you ever derived any enjoyment from them. I will sell your favourite books and delete songs you have downloaded. In order to reconnect and fight against my polluting influence you must seek out those things you enjoyed doing before I came along. If that was walking by the river, do it. If it was knitting, dig out the needles again. I will try and prevent you from doing these things but I cannot be there all the time. By resurrecting these enjoyable things from your life prior to me, you will be reconnecting with reality and escaping from the false reality I have trapped you in. You will feel a sense of self again and begin peeling yourself away from me. I will hate this. I want to subsume you into me and take on your attributes for my own, stripping you of them. Anything which smacks of you asserting a separate self from me alarms me in the extreme and yes I will fight back to try and prevent you from taking these steps, but if you maintain committed to returning to your old delights and reconnecting your social support networks, you will find that I am unable to exert my hold over you for much longer.

# Withdrawal

Within our relationship I use the technique of withdrawal (some call it withholding) to further my control and abuse of you. Having secured your dependence on me by the lavishing of affection I will then no longer feel the need to do so any longer. I can withdraw from you and you still pour admiration my way in an effort to hold onto me. By subjecting you to withdrawal, you experience a huge sense of loss, which conversely provides me with fuel and delivers a delicious high for me. The form in which my withdrawal takes place is numerous. The foremost method is allied to silent treatment where I in effect disappear from your life for a period of time. You may not know where I am or if you do, you are unable to contact me as I have changed telephone number or I will not answer your telephone calls, your texts or emails. This withdrawal varies in length; it may be a few hours or it may be a few weeks. If I am able to observe your attempts to contact me, the text messages and the missed calls, then this is furnishing me with attention and consequently fuel. How should you escape the effects of my withdrawal?

1.      I will return. I have to do this, as I want to extract fuel from you. My withdrawal does not work without me returning to you as if nothing has happened. I want to waltz back in, probably accompanied by some grandiose gesture and ready to drink deep at the fountain of your fuel as you burst into tears of joy and gratitude at my return. Few things taste as sweet as your relief.

2.      No matter how long it may feel like I am away for and it may suggest that it is permanent, I will come back. I have to. I have too much invested in you and withdrawal is not discarding you. It is a temporary state of affairs. The extent of how temporary it is will vary, but it is temporary. You must keep that in your mind.

3.      Since I will return there is nothing to be gained in trying to contact me. I want you to chase after me. I want to hear your sob-filled voicemails. I want to read the heartfelt texts. It is showering me with the attention that I crave. Do not chase after me. Make one call and leave one message showing you are able to demonstrate that you care. Thus you discharge your caring obligation and can satisfy yourself that you have behaved appropriately. You then know in your mind you did the correct thing. It also means I cannot then level at you, on my return the accusation that you did not care in a manner you know could be regarded as true.

4.      By chasing after me you are using up your time and energy. You are making yourself anxious and giving me what I want to see and hear. I positively revel in seeing you banging on the door and crying in order to see me. If you do not do it, I gain nothing from the withdrawal and I will return pretty quickly. I am not going to stay away if I am not getting my fuel from you, so I may as well return.

5.      Once I realise that you are not reacting to this form of withdrawal, I will use it less often if at all. I am no fool and as I repeatedly make mention, I do not like to waste my energy. If something is not providing me with fuel, I stop that method and seek out another. My withdrawal has

prompted no reaction in you. In fact, I can see you getting on with your life without me and that pains me. I feel rejected and unwanted so I have to come crawling back.

6.      I explained how I would return feeling triumphant and acting as if nothing has happened. Turn that around. When I do return, smile and greet me and then go back to your book or preparing dinner or whatever else you were doing. Why don't you carry on like nothing has happened? It will soon take the wind from my sails.

7.      Accordingly, when I do my disappearing act, no matter how anxious it makes you feel, do not pander to my attention seeking. Make the one call or send one message and then carry on as normal. I will soon be back and you will have avoided causing yourself anxiety, caused me to feel pain and you will have maintained the upper hand.

A different form of withdrawal, which I deploy, is the removal of affection. As you will be fully aware, during the love-bombing phase I showered you with blissful, dizzying affection. I made love to you often and repeatedly with great attention and orgasmic results. All of this is very addictive. I know this so I will withdraw that affection from you. Whereas I was once the willing Olympian lover, I show no interest in going to bed with you other than to sleep. You reach out a hand to try and draw me close and I shrug it away. I know this really hurts you. I will no longer hold you in bed but instead I will turn my back on you or go and sleep in the spare room.

As with everything I do, this is calculated to draw a reaction from you. It is another form of control. The giving and withholding of affection is in my gift and you will understand that. I will be affectionate if I want something and then take it away again to exert control over you. One of your immediate reactions to this behaviour is to be upset. This is understandable. You will also want to find out what is wrong. Have you done something to upset me? This is what I want. I want you puzzled and pestering me for answers.

Once you have realised that my withholding of affection is one of my many manipulative techniques you know how to best protect yourself.

1.      Hide your upset. This is difficult as everyone craves affection. Understand that I only gave you affection so I could later take it away. The initial affection was not real. This is difficult to grasp but you must do so. If you do not react when I remove the affection, then you have denied me fuel.

2.      I will immediately reinstate the affection because this draws a reaction from you. You are pleased and admire me once again. This will be a temporary state of affairs however as I will try the technique again. Should you not provide any reaction to the withdrawal I may try a number of other times until I get a reaction. If you are content to be subjected to this yo-yo behaviour and are able to do so without it troubling you, since you know what it is, then so be it. You have gained the upper hand.

3.     This will not persist however. For the most part my kind and me find affection and intimacy abhorrent and only engage in it to facilitate the withdrawal and the provision of fuel thereafter. If it is not producing anything, then we are content to not bother eventually. You will be spared the push and pull behaviour but you will find yourself in a relationship (if it is one you cannot leave), which is devoid of this affection. You may reach the conclusion that you are content with that state of affairs as it is preferable to the up and down nature of when I provide you with affection and then without warning remove it. No matter how hard you try, as an empathic individual, having affection removed from you, even when you know why, is still difficult to deal with.

4.     If you are made of stern stuff you may decide to play me at my own game and provide me with a fake reaction to the withdrawal and pretend to be upset. This will take some skill as I am adept at reading people and if I sense your reaction is manufactured I will stop. If you are able to hoodwink me however, you may be able to cause me to provide you with affection, ride the subsequent withdrawal and feign distress so that eventually the affection is returned. I could appreciate that after everything I have done to you, you may wish to engage in such a perverse behaviour just to ensure you receive the affection as you manage the withdrawal.

5.     Many relationships move to a period where the expression of affection is less obvious. You may decide that you are content to have the relative calm that comes with that. You will trade avoiding the upset for an

absence of affection. This is you gaining control and one method of managing my manipulative technique of withdrawal.

# Threatened Loss

Threatened loss is where I cause you to fear that you will lose me and lose our relationship. I have convinced you of the validity of the golden period and as a consequence you are concerned that if you do not do as I wish, you will lose this.

The difficulty you have is that you are dealing with someone who does not think in the same way that you do. You do not know whether I will actually act out the threat of taking something away from you. Accordingly, the most appropriate way to deal with this is to always take the threatened loss at face value. There is no point trying to second-guess me. I will not follow logic and you may decide that my threat is merely a bluff, only to then find I have acted on it with terrible consequences. By trying to second-guess you will be adding a further layer of anxiety to your position. Does he mean it? Can I gauge whether this is an empty threat? He threatened to end things last time but he did not, is he acting the same way this time as he was then? Is anything different? You will tie yourself up in knots. Instead, treat every threat at face value, this way you can decide how best to deal with it. Ignoring it is unwise.

Many of my threats are knee-jerk reactions but that does not diminish the risk of me carrying them out. Since they are knee-jerk in nature it makes it difficult for you to ascertain whether it is empty or not. Treat each threat as serious. By threatening you I am trying to take control of your decision-making process for you. By treating each threat as real you are maintaining control over your decision-making.

You must always act on the threat. If I threaten to hurt you or someone else, involve the police. By doing this you reduce the risk of escalation. If I threaten to break something or steal something, move that item away from where I might find it. If I threaten to take money, transfer the money to somewhere that I cannot access. If I threaten to end the relationship if you do not do as I want, then you need to prepare for that eventuality. By always treating my threats seriously you are conveying to me that you are doing so and in turn this will cause me to realise that you are making me accountable for my actions. I have explained on many occasions that I dislike accountability as I do not regard myself as someone who should be beholden to anybody else. By demonstrating that my threat is being taken seriously, you are telling me that any outcome arising from my threat is down to me. This may have the effect of causing me to think twice about following the threat through. I would much rather avoid having to contemplate accountability and not perform the threatened action, than carry out and be stuck with feeling responsible for this.

Never goad me or try to call my bluff. This will only escalate the situation. Whereas I have explained that you can make feel accountable and this may reduce the likelihood of me carrying out the threatened behaviour, goading me or inviting me to do it, just to test me, is dangerous. In this situation you are challenging me. I do not like to be challenged. I will thus carry out the threat and I will also be able to blame you for making me do it (thus absolving me of any responsibility). This is exactly what I want. I blame you, I feel no responsibility and I carry out the threat.

Do not be concerned that others may think that you are over-reacting to my threat. They are not the ones facing my threat, you are. You must focus on your own position and not be concerned about how others may regard it. As I have advised, you should avoid becoming bogged down in second-guessing my intentions, do not fall into the trap of wondering how other people might react. That is irrelevant. It is happening to you and not to them.

# Character Assassination

The Character Assassination and its larger cousin, the Smear Campaign are regularly used by me. I utilise them during the devaluation phase by telling untruths to other people about you. Part of this tactic is to ensure that this gets back to you for me to then deny it. You are unsure what to believe. Why would someone who loves you the way I do say such a nasty thing about you? I would not do that would I? It is obviously untrue or your friend is trying to cause trouble between us. This serves the purpose of isolating you (see above) and also implementing gas lighting as you become unsure of your reality. I am also doing this during the devaluation phase so that when I eventually discard you and you go running to other people to complain about my abhorrent treatment you will be met with,

"Yeah, sure he did," and "whatever you say."

With people pointing to their heads behind your back to suggest you have some kind of mental health problem.

I will also carry out this activity during the discard phase to justify why I no longer wish to be with you. The tales of your abusive behaviour towards me and your legendary histrionic hissy fits will be spread far and wide. This also helps me when I am targeting somebody else as you are made out to be the jealous and crazy ex-girlfriend so if you try and warn my new prey about me they will just regard you as envious and dismiss what you say. You will be left in a Kafkaesque nightmare of trying to convince everyone you are right and I am wrong, when I have already got there first.

How then do you tackle this nasty form of abuse?

The most important thing to understand is that you have little control over what other people think. People object to being told how to view a situation. They like to think they have their own mind (even though they adopt a herd mentality) and they want to reach their own conclusions (or think that they do). You have even less chance of controlling the thoughts of people who I have brainwashed. Don't waste your energy trying. Do not allow yourself to be anxious about what these people think. It is difficult but you must keep reminding yourself that you know the truth and if they cannot see it, that is their problem not yours.

Consider whether you would really want to be involved with these people anyway. Consider why do their opinions mean so much to you? Chances are, on reflection you will realise that their opinions are meaningless and it is the fact that something untrue has been said about you which is troubling you. Being the empath that you are, you want to set the record straight. You have to resist this temptation as it will cause you more trouble that it is worth.

Keep in mind that I will know that you are rushing around trying to tell people I am the problem and that it is not you. This is giving me the fuel. The knowledge that I am hurting you, that you are upset and that you are going around talking about me is exactly what I want. Stop it. You will save yourself much anxiety and you will immediately deprive me of something I want. This will give you a sense of control over the situation.

Do not blame yourself in any way. You may be tempted, by reason of your inwardly reflective and pleasant nature, to feel that you are in some way responsible for the things that I am saying about you. Perhaps if you had tried harder or done something differently then I would not be saying these things. Do not delude yourself. Whatever you have or have not done is irrelevant. I will manufacture anything to smear your name. By accepting blame, you are allowing me to exert further control over you and once more you are giving me fuel. Do not hold yourself to account for the savage and unpleasant ramblings of someone who is disordered.

Ensure you spend time with those who are on your side. This will give you validation and strength. Do not preoccupy yourself with the impossible task of converting those who will never listen to you and instead bask in the support of those who are allied with you. You will feel better about yourself and they will distract you from thinking about what I am saying about you.

Do not try and 'get me back' for what I am saying. You will not succeed and I want a reaction from you. You are merely giving me further fuel by responding to my antagonism. Rise above it.

If the nature of the assassination is especially unpleasant and is done through social media, you may wish to consider reporting the behaviour to the relevant provider or even the police for appropriate action to then be taken. Whilst this is an option, it does provide me with some form of attention and reaction and you may find the better course is just to ignore what I am doing. The right-minded people will not believe me and those who do believe what I say are not worth you bothering with. I hate being ignored and this is a prime occasion for you to do just that.

# Obsessing

Causing you to obsess is another of our methods of control. You will scrutinise the things I have said and done and try to work them out. You will analyse your own behaviour to try and work out whether something you have done has caused that reaction in me. You become anxious, hyper-vigilant, stuck and confused. It is an utter waste of your time and energy, yet you fall into doing it with the greatest of ease. Why is that?

You are programmed to want to know why people do as they do. You derive pleasure, in an entirely healthy manner, from understanding what makes people tick. This then enables you to do what you do best; care for them, take an interest in them and derive joy from their joy. This is all very admirable. Regrettably, we know that your desire for answers and understanding may drive you into obsessing over details. You need to understand why we act as we do. Why did we make that remark? What was behind that comment? Why did I not call you back? You have become aware that I have gone out with an old flame and you need to know whether we are just friends or is there something more sinister to it? We push you into this state of obsessing over the relationship because we have conditioned you to second guess our behaviour. If I do this, will he get angry? If I do that, will it please him? Once upon a time (before your involvement with me) you would do things and nine times out of ten you would get the expected response. That was because you were dealing with sensible and healthy people. Then I came along.

You might want to return to an earlier chapter where I wrote about Logic and have those comments fixed in your mind as you consider this section. My reactions to the things you would do never seemed to have any grounding in logic did they? I would fly into a rage because you took the last slice of bread (even though I had already remarked that I was full). That reaction made no sense. I said I was full, thus implying I did not want any more and you also knew that I had eaten several more slices than you, thus suggesting that I might then not be entitled to that last slice. Not in my world. My disproportionate reaction to a trivial matter causes you to then begin second guessing me. I think he is asleep so if I take him a cup of tea and wake him he will be angry. What if he is not asleep and waiting for a cup of tea in bed, he will be angry with me for not taking one to him. If I go and check if he is asleep or waiting for a drink and I disturb him that may make him angry. Does this sound familiar? If you asked your pre-me self to read that that is how you will end up behaving, you would shake your head and laugh. But it happens. It always happens.

By causing you to second guess our behaviour we also lead you down the path of obsessing over everything that goes on in our relationship. You become hyper vigilant to it, trying to read the signs and fathom out what really is going on. This is exhausting and ultimately fruitless.

There is a further reason why we like to engender in you the behaviour of obsessing. Yes, it provides us with fuel, that is our primary objective, but also if you are spending your time trying to work and figure things out, you are going nowhere. You are taking no action and you are just stuck in the same place. We like that. It means we can get on with what we want to do in the full knowledge that you will be still sat there trying to work out if our last comment about "needing to spend more time with your friends" was a coded death knell for the relationship. We do not want you to work things out. We do not want you taking action. We want you sat there, obsessing, anxious and static.

In tackling my use of causing you to engage in obsessing, you need to keep the following in mind.

1. Understand that when you are doing this you are sub-consciously fuelling your affection for me. By repeatedly thinking about me and why I have done or said something causes you to increase your affection because of who you are. You do not feel it as affection because the anxiety engulfs that sensation. This is what is happening beneath the worry.

2. Regain perspective. Does the fact that I left without saying good bye actually matter? Once upon a time you will have shrugged it off and you will have not been concerned by it. The gradual and steady erosion of your ability to cope means that you will be worried that it may mean that I am unhappy with you. Then again it may not. You could try and find out by ringing me up to ask but then you are playing straight into my hands. I have done this on purpose because

I know you will be wondering what it means. We know that you obsess and we play on it as part of our manipulation of you. The thought of you sat at home or at work, concerned about this lack of farewell makes us feel powerful. Look at the effect we have on you by omitting a simple good bye. If you telephone us to ask, you are giving us even more attention and we love it. Stand back for a moment and ask yourself this question,

"Does it really matter?"

The answer will invariably be no.

3. Ask yourself what am I achieving by doing this? If you are analysing something you have said or done, it has already happened. It cannot be changed. Move on. My kind and me never sit and concern ourselves with what has happened. We regard such regular introspection and reflection as work and unproductive. We have to move forward. Always forward. You are sitting in the past which is completely pointless. If you are scrutinising my behaviour remind yourself that trying to figure my kind and me out is a difficult and often fruitless task. Logic is thrown from the window. Your time is better spent reading this book and ones like it than trying to work us out on your own.


4. Find a direct no-nonsense friend who will act as your filter. Every time you wish to scrutinise something that I have done, raise it with

this person. They will not soothe you like some friends will by listening and analysing with you (what good is that?) instead they will be blunt and tell you to stop being so silly and ignore it. You may protest but they will not entertain you discussing it for another syllable. Make sure you turn to this person and not someone who enables you to sit and scrutinise everything.

5. Following on from the above do not also obsess with other friends who are content to allow you to do it. You are bypassing the friend at four above and undoing their good work. Moreover, these friends are not helping. They have the best of intentions. They will sit and listen, offer advice and sympathise. They will enjoy trying to fathom out my behaviour. They will come to expect you to sit down with them or ring and say, "He has done x, what does it mean?" They want you to come to them with the next piece of the jigsaw. Much as they want to help you, they are also getting something from this situation being perpetuated and it is not helping you. Do not turn to these friends.

6. You have formed a habit of obsessing and you actually derive enjoyment from doing it as it gives you something to talk about with an enabling friend. Although it causes you anxiety, you have become reliant on turning to a friend or standing talking to yourself in a

mirror. You enjoy doing it as you remain hopeful of determining an answer, because as I mentioned at the beginning of this section, you need an answer that makes sense. I will tell you again, we do not operate normally or logically. You will not find an answer which satisfies your need for logic and understanding so do not waste time and energy trying to find it.

7. If you find stopping obsessing altogether far too difficult, discipline yourself to only spend fifteen minutes each day considering my actions. This zone must take place at the same time each day and for the same amount of set time. If you find yourself obsessing outside of the zone, you must stop and reserve the activity for the allotted time. Over time reduce the allowed time for obsessing until it becomes zero.

8. Fill your time with other things to reduce the time available for indulging in obsessing.

9. Train yourself to realise you have started obsessing and then to train yourself to go and do something else. This takes time and discipline but you ought to do it.

10. Avoid any kind of stalking behaviour which you may think will get you answers. Especially avoid the habit of cyber stalking. This will just throw fuel onto your obsessing as odds on you will see something which raises more questions than it answers.


11. Why are you trying to become an expert in understanding someone who hurts you? Would you not be better off investing that time in you, rather than me?

# Silent Treatment

This is a staple method of manipulation we use. It is devastating in its effect as it will leave you confused, withdrawn, isolated and a changed person. Whereas once you were vivacious and outgoing, this systematic form of abuse has left you a broken shell of a person who no longer wants to go out or do anything. In its most obvious form we just ignore you. Often we do this by leaving you and going somewhere else, usually without telling you where, so you are not able to contact us. We may use it in other ways by talking on the telephone to other people but refusing to speak to you. Or in a family situation, we will speak to everyone in that family at a gathering save one. One of the most effective ways I utilised it was to arrange a special dinner at an excellent restaurant. My victim would be excited about going out and will have been looking forward to it. Once we were seated I would not speak. I am so cold-hearted I could sit there as she looked at me with incredulity and increasing distress as I just sat and stared back at her without saying anything. I knew that the relevant victim would not cause a scene and therefore would be trapped trying to pretend to those waiting on us and the diners nearby that nothing was wrong, all the while she would be hissing whispers across at me asking what was wrong and what had she said? The people I did this to always left the restaurant in tears and thus I secured a huge dose of fuel. Horrible behaviour I know but I need to get that fuel.

It is massively effective. We love it because it takes such little effort to do but has such an impact because whilst you find the silence irritating it is the reason why we are doing this to you that causes you the most consternation. There it is again; the empath's need to know.

Why do we use silent treatment? There are several reasons for this

- We want you to give us more attention by asking us what is wrong
- We use it as a form of manipulation to make you do something that we want
- We want to hurt you by making you bewildered and confused as to why we are treating you in this fashion
- We have lost control of a discussion and this is the only way we know how to regain control. We are in effect sulking like a child
- We wish to avoid responsibility for a situation. If we do not discuss it with you, we are not responsible for it
- Boundary testing. We want to see how far we can push you

In the context of a relationship, our silent treatment manifests in two ways. Firstly, through the deployment of what is a present silence. We will remain in the home with you but we will just not speak to you. Often we will subject you to a cold, hard stare (by adding in some intimidation to the mix) and remain silent. We will speak to other people on the telephone, other members of the household and those who attend the house in order to exacerbate our treatment of you. The second type is absent silence. This is where we will leave the house and go and stay somewhere else. It may be that I have kept a property on even though we have moved in together or spend most of our time at your property, so I have a bolt hole to return to. I may have given you keys to this property but I will ensure that I deadbolt the door to frustrate you. I disappear and you know where I have gone to. That is designed on purpose. You think you can get in but I prevent you from doing so and thus I increase your sense of helplessness. In some ways, the absent silence is easier to deal with. Once you realise I will return (see my comment below) you are able to carry on without my spectral presence hanging over you. Whereas if I maintain a present silence it is very wearing being in the same place as someone who will not speak to you, or so I have witnessed.

How do you go about dealing with our silent treatment of you?

1. At the beginning of the silent treatment you can point out to us that you know what we are doing and invite us to discuss it with you. If we have remained in the home with you, you can speak to us and do it in a calm fashion. This is not giving us an emotional reaction. If

we have absented ourselves send a text message or put a note through the door. In either case, only do this the once. You have discharged your sense of obligation to behave as an emotionally mature person and will feel better for it. You cannot (legitimately although of course we may still try to) be accused of not caring. It is unlikely to stop the silent treatment but once in a while it just might. If it does not, then you can rest easy knowing you have reacted in the most appropriate fashion to try and resolve the silence, without giving us the emotional reaction we crave. If the silence persists it is time to move on to the following stages.

2. Ignore us. If you carry on as normal, we instantly see that the silent treatment has not worked. We may switch of course to a different form of manipulation but since we want a reaction from you and none is forthcoming, we will stop. Accordingly, if we have remained in the home with you and are not speaking to you but to others, do not lose your temper or show any distress. Instead carry on as normal. If we have absented ourselves from the home, you may wish to satisfy yourself that you know we are safe by checking. If that puts your mind at rest, then do so and then wait until we come back to you. Don't keep trying to contact us. By sending text messages, issuing posts on social media, telephoning and try to see us you are providing us with fuel. This will just make us prolong the silent treatment.

3. Be aware that we are using it to test you and we will return. In common with normal people, you do not like a situation where you

do not know the outcome. If you have no idea whether or not I will return to you, this causes you anxiety. Understand that we will return. We need to in order to obtain fuel from you. Since you are the person we have chosen, you are the most obvious and easiest way for us to obtain that fuel. We need to return to you and we will. It may feel uncomfortable since it will feel like you are venturing into the unknown but we will return.

4. Keep in mind that we like to push the boundaries. If the first bout of absenteeism lasted a week before I returned, then the second bout is likely to last longer than a week. We do this because if you learn from the experience you may tell yourself, "Oh, he was gone a week. He has gone again; he will be back in a week I guess." We realise that you think this and therefore we will purposefully extend the silent treatment through absence beyond the initial stage of a week in order to make you think that we are not coming back this time as it has been longer. This is just another tactic designed to have you come running to try and get us back and in turn provide us with that much needed fuel.

5. Do not challenge us or lose your temper. This is what we want to happen and this will just stiffen our resolve to continue with the silent treatment.

6. Do not attempt to try and find out what is wrong. There is nothing wrong that you can fix because it is not something you have done that merits this type of response. In my mind I will have some sleight occasioned by you (often imagined rather than real) or it will

be a completely disproportionate response to a real event (such as crumbs in the butter resulting in a major meltdown).

7. Do not soothe or placate. We want this and since you are giving us what we want we will keep on doing it for longer and repeatedly as it is effective.

8. Do not enlist the help of others to try and persuade us to talk to you. This is fuel to us but also we will use it as a stick to beat you with when we return by lambasting you for involving other people in our business. Generally, outside of the home we do not want people to know that we are doing this to you as it dents our perfect image, so we will ensure that any step taken which broadcasts this will be met with a fierce reaction when we do return and/or resume talking to you.

9. Use the time away from our behaviour, if we have opted for an absent silence to focus on you. Gather some strength and enjoy the respite.

10. With normal people who may have chosen silence as a way of dealing with a difficult situation it is often suggested that you offer an olive branch so they can climb down from the silence without losing face, otherwise they may feel they have nowhere to go and thus they are compelled to continue with it. This will not work with us. We will see any attempt (no matter how well framed and well intentioned) as weakness on your part and amounting to giving us attention. Avoid doing this.

11.     Do not think that some dramatic plea or act will shake us from our silence. If you hurt yourself in a bid to make us engage or threaten to do so, it will not work. Not only are you giving us fuel but we do not feel any empathy for your situation. Instead we will use your behaviour to validate our own. "Yes I was not speaking to her because she kept going on at me. She is crazy. Look at what she ended up doing, is it any wonder I left?"

12.     When we re-engage with you (and we will) in healthy relationships you would be encouraged to discuss what has happened and for the person exhibiting the silent treatment to be held accountable for their behaviour. There is no point in attempting this with us as we will deny we have done anything wrong and blame shift on to you. There is no point in engaging. No matter how much you want to point out to us how immature and pathetic our silence has been and how hurtful this behaviour is when we act in this fashion, in order to disarm the effectiveness of this behaviour you must resist the urge to engage with us in this fashion. Act like nothing has happened. This will annoy us but will also show to us that the act of adopting silence does not work with you, at its start, during it and at its conclusion.

# Ever presence

Ever presence is a particularly insidious manipulative technique that I use. It is different from the other forms of manipulation as it is a lasting legacy from our relationship and is embedded in your life. It becomes active and effective when either I have discarded you or when you have decided to leave me. My aim is always to gain your attention and thus fuel. To achieve this, I need you to be thinking about me often and repeatedly. When I love bombed you, I did this by appearing as often as I could, text messaging you, telephoning and posting messages to you through social media. Each time I 'popped up' you would think of me so that you became conditioned to thinking of me and little or nothing else. Since I know that I am in your head then that will provide me with fuel as you are giving me attention. It also appeals to my sense of omnipotence and makes me powerful.

With Everpresence I ensure that I appear to you everywhere you look and go. I have been ingraining my presence into every facet of your life from the moment I met you. I purposefully ensure that it is associated with all of the best memories and moments of happiness. It is responsible for euphoric recall. You will hear a particular song and immediately remember that time we held one another as a storm thundered over head and you felt safe and cared for. When you hear that song again that wonderful moment will immediately spring into your thoughts and you will feel that familiar surge of delight. When you have been discarded, you will engage in this to make yourself feel better by remembering the golden parts of our relationship. Each time you do, you make it harder to escape its effect. You will need to take responsibility for your own desire to keep dipping into these moments. You will be addicted to doing so because you are feeling low and upset, finding anything that will make you feel better, even if it is for a just a short time it is relief from the pain. Indulging in euphoric recall when it has been triggered will only ultimately make the pain for you worsen.

If you have decided to get away from me, I want you to experience that sensation of euphoric recall. You may be able to discipline yourself to not sit in contemplation of our wonderful times together and thus deny the appearance of this euphoric recall. In order to counter that, I need the sensation to happen without you realising. Accordingly, I link it to smells, sounds, tastes and sights. Everywhere you look you will be reminded of me and automatically a sense of euphoria will be recalled as you smell my after shave again and it makes you remember how you felt so good when you used to bury your head in my chest. It is a truly potent method of continuing to manipulate you. It is done so that when I decide to try and hoover you back in in, you will be far more susceptible to me doing so. Furthermore, I know that you will be afflicted by this method of manipulating you. You will be thinking of me and this provides me with fuel, power and omnipotence.

Tackling ever presence is especially difficult as it is always linked to good and pleasant things. You are going to have to make certain sacrifices to prevent it from working. This is not about avoiding me (that comes under no contact) it is about removing anything that might trigger a memory of me and thus euphoric recall about me. Some of these steps may not be practical for you or are prohibitive for financial reasons and in those instances you may consider trying to achieve a similar effect of deleting me from the scenario or changing the scenario so it is less inclined to remind you of me. With other instances it is more about being ruthless in your need to purge my ever presence from your life. There is no room for sentiment. Everything must go to enable you to combat this manipulative technique.

- Photographs. Burn all of the photographs that I appear in. Remove them from all social media, mobile phones, PCs, laptops and tablets. Yes, you may look fantastic in that picture with me (I am sure you can alter it so you are preserved and I am not). As you remove the pictures say "I delete you (say my name)" and this process of exorcising me from a visual part of your life will feel uplifting.

- All gifts, mementos, cards, letters and those little trinkets that we so often send one another must be removed. Burn them, shred them and dispose of them. Where possible, sell certain items and you will gain increased satisfaction from having made some money out of it too.

- Do not fall into the trap of thinking that you are exhibiting strength by carrying on and still wearing a bracelet that I bought you to show me that you think more of the bracelet than me. That will not work. I will see the bracelet and think, "Ah, she still wears it. She cannot bear to part with it. She obviously thinks of me still." You do not think like that but I do and thus I will draw fuel from it and also think that I have a chance to draw you back in. You need to be ruthless.

- Stop going to the places we went together. It does not matter that they serve great pizza, plenty of other places do as well. Regard it as an opportunity to create new memories in new places.

- Consider going away for a long weekend or a week in order to reset your routine.

- Again, do not be tempted to still go to these places with someone new or even on your own to prove you can do it without me. I will be checking the places that we frequented to see if I can see you there (especially if you have tried to get away from me) in order to try and draw you back in again and provide me with some more fuel. Consequently, all you are doing is giving me fuel and suggesting to me I can reel you back in. I will view it as you being unable to stop going because it reminds you so much of me.

- Music. Delete those 'special' songs. Sell the CDs. Get rid of the play lists.

- Have no connection to me through social media. Generally speaking, you should deactivate your social media in order to escape me because it is such a potent method of enabling me to keep tabs on you and try to communicate with you.

- Stop any conversations about me. If someone else brings up my name, politely point out that you no longer discuss or consider me and change the topic. Your closest friends will have most likely done this automatically and other friends and acquaintances will soon learn to do this too.

- When an anniversary looms ensure you have organised to do something else, utterly unrelated to me and with people who will keep you entertained and distracted. Before long the dates will pass by without you noticing.

- Remove films and books that act as triggers. Again sell them. Do not watch them again. Change channel if they appear on television unexpectedly.

- Remove any fragrances or scents that you associate with me. Most will have been personal to me but you may still have some that the smell of then immediately places me in the room - it might be shower gel, a scented candle or air freshener. Change them and experience some new ones.

- You may contemplate changing jobs if we worked at the same company or business. Naturally this is a significant change on your part but if you find that my presence does linger in the work place (even if I do not work there any more) and you are able to do so without too great a difficulty, then change job.

- Move house. If we lived together you will see me sat in a certain chair, stood at a particular window or soaking in the bath. This is also a drastic step and may not be practical but if it helps erase my memory and prevent triggers then I recommend you do this also. If moving house is not an option, consider rearranging the furniture so rooms look different, buy new furniture, purchase different cushions and bedspreads and/or re-decorate. Making these changes will underline you feeling of a new beginning and the discarding of an old toxic environment. Occupying yourself with selecting colours and fabrics will also distract you from thinking about me and ultimately seeing my ghost around your house

- Avoid socialising with those people you know are connected to me. You may also get rid of a Lieutenant or two of mine at the same time.

Along with deleting as many potential triggers as possible so as to extinguish or diminish my everpresence you can also look to dilute it. By entering into new relationships, doing different activities and making new friends you will be removing yourself from these triggers. You will also be distracted by these new things. You are less likely to find the triggers in these new places and you will be better able to cope with the few that do arise.

Tackling everpresence in this way is not a complete solution however since there is always a risk that a certain song will be playing in the background when you go somewhere or it comes on the radio. Yes, you can switch off the radio or you may be able to leave the place where it is being played, but by then it has already resurrected the memory. The advantage you do have is that by applying the techniques listed above, you will have been able to lessen the amount of euphoric recall you are subjected to. This means that it will have less of an effect. Additionally, since you are not subjected to it as often, you will be able to build up your own resistance to it, so that if you are inadvertently exposed to something that will trigger euphoric recall, you will be less inclined to indulge in it and remain exposed to it and you will then take steps to counter it.

Alter your environment through new additions and ruthless removals and you will succeed in diminishing and ultimately escaping my tendrils that are extended through everpresence.

# Bringing up the Past

We like to do this as a method of denial and deflection. Remember in any argument we will never accept any responsibility for what we have said and done. We believe we are not accountable to anyone and we are not to blame for anything. In order to preserve this state of mind, even when confronted by an incontrovertible fact we will look to go on the attack and shift the focus of the blame onto you. One method of doing this is to bring up the past. We also deploy this method to let you know that anything you do or say can and will be used against you in the future. It is a further method of control and is done to ensure that you are walking on eggshells.

We are experts at remembering every single thing that you will have done that we find offensive. Our power of recall is formidable when it comes to you and your misdemeanours (but surprisingly less so when it involves remembering something we have done or something important in your life). In bringing up the past we will: -

- Resurrect the 'biggest' fault or problem you caused

- Bring up minor matters which are barely worth remembering

- Bring up matters which are irrelevant to the discussion in hand

- Invent transgressions on your part in order to confuse and infuriate

- Ignore the fact that the point we are bringing up was actually resolved

If we can use it to blame you, we will dig it up and throw it at you.

How should you deal with this?

1.     Do not engage the accusation. As an empathic individual you like things to be correct. You do not like to be accused of something that you did not do, is irrelevant or you have already apologised and atoned for. It offends you mightily if this is brought up. This is why we do it as you always struggle to avoid it and instead address it head on in your crusade to establish correctness. You become so distracted in defending yourself that you lose sight of the original part of the discussion (all part of the plan) and find yourself dragged into a discussion about your behaviour. Resist the urge to respond to it.

2.     Do not respond in an aggressive fashion. This is what we want. A reaction. One of my former girlfriends would say,

"I realise that point still concerns you but that is not what is being discussed" in a calm and polite manner and she would then proceed to return the discussion to the previous topic.

If you respond with comments such as

"Oh God, not that old chestnut"

"Seriously, that was like ten years ago?"

"Here we go again, how many times have I had to say sorry for selling your collection of marbles, they weren't worth much anyway."

"That's right, drag up the past, you always do this when you know I am right."

You are showing that we have got under your skin with the manner of your response, the hands on hips and pursed lips. This will make us keep going in order to maintain you fuelling us.

3.    Shut down the attempt. Another of my girlfriends would say,

"We discussed that at length and resolved it. Now let's resolve this issue" and then return straight to the relevant topic. By avoiding any criticism or rancour at our dragging up the past and instead blocking it firmly and calmly, we can see it is not gaining any reaction from you.

4.    Where I have invented something, again if you react to it by declaring

"What on earth are you talking about, you are making that up. You always do this."

You are giving me the reaction you want. You need to address this attempt to provoke you by meeting it firmly and in a controlled manner. The girlfriend above, Paula I think, used to respond by saying

"We are not discussing that at present we are discussing…" and then continue with the topic. By denying the validity of what I have said by failing to engage in it, you remove the energy from the situation.

5.    If necessary end the conversation and explain that it is clear a meaningful discussion cannot take place. Do so in a reasonable manner

and then point out that you need to go out or attend to some chores so you do not give the impression of having stormed away as we will use that to satisfy ourselves that you have given us the reaction we wanted. Instead, if you bring the futile discussion to a close in a sensible fashion, the energy is dissipated and we have not got what we want. We will remember this and thus become less likely to deploy this technique in the future with you.

# Boundary Violations

Our massive sense of entitlement means that we believe we can do as we want, go where we want and treat people in any fashion we see fit without any concern for a repercussion. This reinforces that we do not value you in anyway, it tells you that whatever is yours is also ours and that you cannot complain about such behaviour since it has no validity. It was ours to begin with so why are you complaining? Domestic theft is a classic example of how we violate boundaries. We will take a shared resource and appropriate it entirely for our needs without any thought for anybody else in the household. An example would be blowing the food budget on a night out or drinking all of the soda so nobody else can have any even though it is a hot day. Should you complain about this we will give you a blank look. It belonged to us, so how can you possibly criticise us for this? Oh, yes, you like to have a go at us don't you? This is just typical behaviour from you, finding fault with me when it is down to you. Straight into some blame shifting after we have trampled all over that boundary.

How else do these boundary violations manifest?

- Intruding on your privacy

- Interrupting you when you have asked to be left alone

- Breaching confidentiality and revealing secrets when we have been asked not to

- Flirting with people despite you having asked us not to do this

- Playing loud music when you have explained you have a headache

We do not recognise boundaries in interpersonal relationships. We stand too close to people, get "in their space" and will kiss them on the lips when it is not appropriate to do so. We will not recognise any failing on our part in doing this. We open your post, read your e-mails, listen in on your conversations and turn up uninvited to certain events where it was clear we were not welcome. With the sudden rhino hide we develop in these instances, we park our tank on your lawn, tramp our muddy boots through your house and jump on your bed with a grin and a hello. Point out this behaviour to us and the rhino hide suddenly turns wafer thin and we are mortally aggrieved. It is highly annoying and designed to demean and belittle you.

People convey boundaries verbally by stating no, yes or okay for example. They also communicate boundaries in a non-verbal fashion by tone, facial expression, hand gestures and stance. It shows the perverted nature of our behaviour because as I have explained in previous publications we are masters of reading body language. In the case of you establishing and trying to maintain a boundary with the use of non verbal signs we see it but we ignore it.

Furthermore, we revel in establishing boundaries for you. We have a high need to control you and will manifest the establishment of boundaries as a method of doing so. You will not go to certain places, you may not go out after a certain time, you may not socialise with a certain group and so on. By making the rules and establishing boundaries for you, we are controlling you and preventing you from backing us into a corner. Our hypocrisy in setting out these rigid boundaries for you whilst flagrantly ignoring any you may establish for us is also designed to draw a reaction from you.

Why do we do this? As with everything it is our need for fuel but what is behind this action? It is because we do not recognise you as a person in your own right. You are just an extension of ourselves and therefore we take anything and everything of yours as we see it as belonging to us. We will not recognise conventions or protocols because we are not accountable to anybody. This failure to see anybody else and our lack of responsibility means that we are the ultimate invaders.

Dealing with our violations of your boundaries is difficult because in most cases it is very difficult to actually stop us doing it. Instead of trying to affect our behaviour, you need to adjust your own to minimise the impact of our violations on you. This falls into two camps. The first is ensuring you do not provide an emotional reaction to the violation.

In a calm fashion you need to explain how the violation makes you feel. For example, you might state

"When you read my post and e-mails I feel disappointed and disrespected. If you keep doing this, I will arrange for my post to be sent elsewhere and change my e-mail account."

You should note that whilst reference is made to how you feel about our violation you have not conveyed it in an emotive manner. This is a key distinction. We feed on your emotional response not a factual response about your emotions. You will feel satisfied because you have been able to assert yourself. You have also, again in a reasoned fashion, laid down a specific step. This step is not punishing us (for example if you had said I am not making you any more meals until you stop doing this - we will regard this as an unfair punishment and it will offend our sense of entitlement). The step is a reasoned response to the violation. It is unlikely to stop us doing it again, because we believe we are entitled to read your post, but you will then feel entirely justified in taking the relevant step on the next occasion we violate that boundary.

The ineffective way to respond would be as follows: -

"I hate it when you read my post and e-mails, you are just a nosey bastard who has to intrude on everything I do. You just don't care about my privacy do you?" and done so whilst shouting you have generated several problems. Firstly, you have given us an emotional response, which is what we crave. Secondly, you have labelled us and blamed us (a nosey intruding bastard) and thirdly you have acted in an accusing manner (saying we do not care). We will not hear the main thrust of your comment, namely that you are annoyed with our boundary violation. All we will focus on is your labelling, blaming and accusing. This will offend our sense of superiority and result in us reacting by unleashing a torrent of rage in your direction. Your response may feel justified but it will not have any effect with us. On the contrary, my kind and me will escalate the situation and all the while we are blaming you for this happening.

The second method of minimising the impact of our behaviour means in effect taking evasive action. In respect of domestic theft, you should consider keeping certain monies separate and hiding items that we are prone to take as our own to the detriment of others. If you find that we have a habit of interrupting you when you have friends over to see you, you may consider moving the gathering to a different venue which we will not know about or having it take place when you know we will be doing something else. Whilst having to take such steps does mean you have to work around us you do have a choice. Either you can do something which may be mildly inconvenient but prevents a further boundary violation or you put up with it keep happening because believe me, we will keep doing it.

# Pity

Pity is a strong technique that we use. It appeals directly to your empathic nature. We are not shouting or being over bearing, nor are we demonstrating any nastiness on this occasion. Instead we are portraying sadness, hurt and despair. All the things we know that you like to cure and mend.

We enjoy deploying pity as a tactic of manipulation. It is useful in the context of when the relationship is ongoing and is extremely useful to us with regards to drawing you back in at a later stage. We use pity because if you pity us you cannot hurt us. Since you are an empathic individual when you pity somebody you cannot take steps that will hurt them because this is contrary to your central beliefs. Yet again we know that. We know that you cannot resist helping people, you want to rush to the aid of someone in difficulty and you want to help people out. You have that inexplicable urge to assist.

We want you to feel sorry for us. On one level we know what we truly are and that frightened and weak creature wants sympathy. We do not like to contemplate this state of affairs and instead take hold of our self-pity and use it as a tool to extract from you what we always want; attention. We are aware that we are using it as a method of control. We can turn pity on and off just as easily as we flick a switch.

We are adept at extracting pity from others so that you will join in the pity party. Cleverly, as part of a smear campaign against you, we will tell others that you are being hurtful towards us and you are trying to do us down. Other people will feel sorry for us and look to you to do something about it. This puts you under a considerable amount of pressure because

- Your primary instinct is to help someone in difficulty

- Other people are standing in judgement of your behaviour, which you do not enjoy

- People feel a need to follow the crowd and the behaviour of others. Since other people feel pity for us, you will also.

By exploiting this dynamic we are aware you will stop whatever hurtful behaviour you are engaging in and pander to our needs. You ought to be aware that pity is one of our key responses to when you opt to apply no contact to us. How many times have you found yourself saying the following?

"I felt sorry for him being on his own, I was always there for him and he was used to that."

"I saw he could not cope on his own. He is not domesticated and I hated to think of him sat alone, not eating properly and feeling sad."

"I know he has done some bad things but he looked so upset, I couldn't stand to see someone that I love looking like that."

"He just looked so miserable if he looks that upset he must love me surely?"

Sound familiar?

You may find it odd that we allow ourselves to use self-pity since doing so is an admission of weakness and inferiority, something we despise and wish to avoid. We deal with our self-pity by blaming our situation on you. You caused this and therefore you owe it to us to put it right. After all, did we not give you so much during the love bombing stage? Of course we ignore the treatment we put you through during devaluation. We also forget about all the love, care and attention you have provided to us previously. That now counts for nothing. What matters is the here and now. We want you to do something for us so we can maintain our control over you. Thus we deploy pity and you then come running to aid us or come running back into our grasp and the dance begins all over again.

We play on being a victim. This need for pity may also be part of triangulation (see below) whereby whilst it is evident that we are the perpetrator and you are the victim, we will make out that you are now the perpetrator of our misery, we are the victim and we will involve a third party to act as rescuer. This will offend your sense of self-sacrifice and wanting to help and will also disorientate you by suggesting that someone else is better placed to attend to our needs. Often we put you in a damned if you do and damned if don't position. You know we are playing the pity card so you do not respond, we then alter the position by engaging it with triangulation and you feel you have to react out of concern that the third party may usurp your position or label you as uncaring. If you give in and respond to our pity, our manipulation of you has worked.

There is no point expressing anger or disgust towards us when we play the victim and seek pity. Your behaviour is giving us attention through your emotional reaction and it also validates our stance.

"Look everyone see how nasty she is to me. I am hurt and she is just being making it worse by calling me names and shouting at me."

Do not justify yourself to us when we are playing the victim. We will not listen in order to make you keep doing it and you are providing us with a reaction. As usual, as an empathic individual who likes to play on the straight and narrow you will feel an overwhelming compulsion to want to set us straight (and anybody else who might be witnessing our behaviour). You must resist this. Do not assume that everyone else believes what we are saying either. Most normal and rational people will realise what we are doing. You have no obligation to explain yourself to others and you should not be wasting your energy doing so.

Do not apologise when you have done nothing wrong. Again this is a reaction and it also shows that our manipulation is working so we will keep doing it.

Do not try harder to please us or help us based on our complaints. Those complaints are either manufactured or our own-fault. You need to disconnect your empathic switch when this behaviour is being displayed.

In such a situation you need to assert just the once what your position is in an unemotional manner and then leave matters. No matter how much we mope around, bleat to other people and harangue you for being uncaring you know you have not been this. Keep in mind it is what you know that matters, not what anyone else (least of all us) might think about you. You have little control over what others may think. Decent people will work it out. The others are not worth bothering about. It is difficult to discipline yourself in this way but by sticking to your position and not indulging in our display of self-pity you are avoiding giving us fuel. You will also avoid the risk of being sucked back into our false reality if you had managed to escape so far.

# Triangulation

Triangulation is a common device that we utilise when we are seeking to control you in order to obtain our supply of fuel. With triangulation we will involve a third element into our relationship in order to cause a number of things. Who or what might this third element be?

- A member of your family or my family

- Your friends or mine

- Colleagues

- Ex-partners (a particular favourite of mine)

- Institutions

- Strangers

- Inanimate objects (cars and mobile phones are common amongst my kind)

By triangulating we confuse you, make you feel anxious and unappreciated. In some instances, we use this third element, when it is a person, to harass and convince you so that you do our bidding. You often fall for this and you do not see that we are utilising a third party to achieve our aims. It may surprise you that someone else will be so susceptible to our instruction to mete out abusive behaviour to somebody else. We are able to achieve this because of our innate superiority.

Consider this. How many times have you done something because someone in a position of authority has asked or told you to do it? Most people have been programmed to obey authority figures all through their lives. It started with their parents, then teachers, lecturers and then their boss. You obey council officials, police officers and doctors. It follows therefore by acting with an air of authority we are able to tap into this sub-conscious behaviour and cause people to do our bidding. Add a layer of our infamous charm and perhaps some other kind of incentive that works for that individual and they will soon do exactly as we ask.

You may be wise to our behaviours but not see them coming through somebody else. If possible, we will use one of our Lieutenants to advance our aims through this triangulation.

In a different method of triangulation, we set you against someone or something and you end up applying your energies trying to defeat the third element rather than actually tackling our behaviour. We often do this where we know someone else is romantically interested in us as well as you (the second person of course having just recently been subjected to a campaign of love bombing). We also do this with family members. We will make one of you the scapegoat and the other the golden child. Now, I do not have children, but I know that my kind regularly utilise this tactic by pitting one sibling against the other. The narcissist will remain at the centre controlling the flow of information and ensuring that the siblings are kept separate from one another and rarely communicate so they do not work out what is being done. One of our type who is a parent wants to keep you isolated and thus they succeed by operating a policy of divide and conquer.

By remaining as the sole source of information the narcissistic parent remains powerful. They also receive two supply lines of fuel. They will aim to drive a wedge between you and your sibling and aim to have you compete with one another for our affection and attention

One of our sweetest most potent forms of fuel is when we know that two people are fighting over us, each trying to outdo the other in order to obtain our approval and appreciation. You may be surprised just how often people fall for this. Of course, it is all linked to the promise of a return to the golden period and since you are so desperate to achieve this you will try to defeat anyone or anything that might prevent you from returning there.

I recruit colleagues, neighbours, family members or people involved in institutions to use them to manipulate you. I will use them as pseudo-rescuers who you think you are able to turn to, for help. The reality is they are feeding back to me what is being said. They are acting out what I plan for you and perpetuate my abuse of you.

The first important part of triangulation is realising that it is happening. Once you have gained this awareness you must keep in mind the following: -

- Just because I am saying it about you does not mean that it is true. Do not begin to believe my lies and propaganda. This is often difficult when you are at low ebb, but you must adopt this stance. Recruit trusted allies to provide you with assistance and strength.

- Do not react in an emotional fashion if I or someone else tells you something that you were not prepared for. It is a central theme in triangulation that lies will be told about you with a view to those lies returning to you, usually from the third party. We want you to erupt into anger or tears on hearing these comments. Remove the energy from them by remaining calm

- Adopt a healthy cynicism to anything I or the third element may say

- Be aware that I will operate several triangles involving you. Once you have uncovered one, bear in mind there are likely to be others.

- Verify comments where you can so you do not make the mistake of attacking or disbelieving someone who is genuine. This will also help you in weeding out our adverse comments.

Your reactions to triangulation are obvious to me.

1.    You will strike out at me, recognising what I am doing by having someone else carry out my abuse of you and that I am pitting you against a third element. This striking out will not bother me in the slightest. It gives me a reaction.

2.    You will try and persuade the third element of the triangle that my behaviour is the problem and it is not you. This reaction on your part also gives me fuel. It is also doomed to failure. The third element is either: -

- Possessed of their own vested interest in wanting me and therefore regards you as the competition

- Brainwashed by me so that your pleas will fall on deaf ears; or

- An inanimate object which oddly enough, you cannot persuade.

You do not have any control over this other person. You need to realise this.

3.	You will submit to the abusive behaviour even further as you become convinced that you are at fault. This may seem unrealistic when viewed dispassionately but believe me, I have seen it happen within the dynamic with an exhausted, confused and shattered victim; or

4.	You depart the triangle.

In defeating my behaviour, you must achieve the fourth item. You have nothing to gain by remaining in this triangle. Identify that you are in such a triangle and then depart from it. The only power you have in this dynamic is over yourself. You cannot control what I do, since I do not operate in the same world of logic as you. There is no appeal to 'our better nature' since we do not have one. We cannot and will not appreciate your point of view since we have no capability for empathy. You are unable to influence the third element for the reasons outlined above. You may feel empowered by telling the other two elements that you know what is happening and you are not engaging in it anymore. The key step you must take in dealing with triangulation is to refuse to engage in it any longer. That is the only response that will work in escaping this form of manipulation.

# Hope

As I mentioned in **Manipulated** we always give you hope. In the relationship you hope that things will change, that we will alter our behaviour and that we will be fixed. The golden period will return and all will be well. When the relationship has ended we maintain a hope that it will begin again by dangling all manner of inducements before you to draw you back in under our control. Again, one of those inducements is the hope that we are genuinely sorry on this occasion, that we have learned the error of our ways and wish to improve. All of this is a false hope.

You need to shift the focus of your hope. Instead of hoping that I will do things to improve and change, hope instead that:

1.    You remain aware of all my manipulative wiles

2.    You find new healthy relationships away from my lieutenants, mannequins and me;

3.    You maintain your resolve to stay away from me

4.    You ensure you have no reason to contact me, look me up or even think about me

5.    You have the strength to delete me from your life and not look back

6.    You maintain your vigilance to head off any attempt to hoover you back in

7.    You keep in mind that I cannot be helped or fixed

8.    You remember that my problems are my problems and not your burden

9.   You remind yourself how terrible my behaviour was and you have no desire or need to be put through that again; and

10.  You have the character to bounce back from this terrible episode in your life.


By focussing your hope on yourself and not me, you stand a far better chance of escaping me.

There is no hope for me. There is hope only for you.

# No Contact

I am ending this book with the behemoth that is the concept of No Contact. I mentioned this briefly in my introduction. You will be well acquainted with the repeated recommendation of applying this technique. That is because it is very effective. My kind and me despise no contact for that very reason. Why is that?

All of our manipulation and abuse is geared to control you. It is to ensure that we are the doers and the decision makers. When you decide to go no contact you are wresting that control away from us. That makes us feel small and impotent. It annoys us as it demonstrates that you are not as useless and inferior as we believe you to be. You are flying in the face of what we have always made you out to be. This is a huge act of defiance in our eyes and one that we cannot stand. You are ignoring us.

Our existence is based on two fundamental tenets. Everything is about us and we are in control. No contact applies a sledgehammer to those concepts and wounds us to the core. Our initial reaction will be one of fury and we will deploy all our tactics to shatter your shield of no contact. We will wheel out every tactic and technique in order to pierce the screen that you have pulled down. Success is paramount. Every day that passes where you maintain no contact sucks away our power and dwindles our potency. Of all the methods available to escape my influence it is the most effective. However, with that effectiveness there comes a price. It is extremely hard to maintain no contact. This is for three reasons.

## A Permanent Connection

Unfortunately for you maintaining no contact is just not a viable option because there is some form of permanent connection between us. Usually it is the fact that we have children together and much as you may like them to have nothing to do with me, you are a decent person and realise that I should have some involvement in their lives. Even if you decide against this I will of course seek redress through the courts. I have not provided in any great detail my behaviour during the judicial process as that is for a different discussion. It will be sufficient to say that engaging me through the court process is not a pleasant experience. Our permanent connection might be because we are neighbours, or that we work together. Alternatively, it may be that I suffer from some illness and if you were to turn your back on me most people would castigate you for doing so (even though it is the correct thing for you to do for the sake of your sanity. Unfortunately, the world still views a physical illness as more real and debilitating than anything mental or psychological. Accordingly, your anxiety, stress and PTSD will fall a distant second to say the fact I am for example suffering from cancer).

The existence of this permanent connection means that you cannot apply the concept of no contact and you are left with trying to minimise contact as best you can. It is in these circumstances where you want to apply no contact but realistically you cannot, that my explanations above about negating and minimising my manipulative techniques have considerable value.

What you must do instead is reduce the potential for me to garner fuel from the interactions we must have. Reduce those interactions to the absolute minimum. When an interaction takes place, if I begin to cause an argument, walk away or end the call. Do not give in to the temptation to 'put me straight' (remember it just will not work with me) or to try and 'make me see sense'. Establish clear boundaries and protocols by which the minimal interaction must take place and stick to them absolutely. Do not deviate.

## My Commitment

Since your decision to implement no contact is a massive affront to my very being, I will utilise every technique I can muster to break this hiatus and establish contact again. Some of the methods I use are as follows: -

- Repeatedly telephoning you. You will have to change your numbers and ensure that I do not get hold of the new ones. Bear in mind I am likely to have established a Lieutenant or two in your circle (often covertly) so they will leak this information to me. In all likelihood it will take several number changes and the loss of some friends to effect this.

- You should also change your mobile phone itself. There is every likelihood that I will have downloaded software onto your mobile phone that allows me to see your texts etc. from my phone that are received and sent from yours. You need to acquire a clean 'phone. I want this information so I can address any potential threats and also to be aware of your movements so I can "bump" into you and endeavour to hoover you back into my world.

- Check that there is not a tracking device fitted to your car. These are usually attached by a magnet to the underside of your vehicle. You would do well to check your car each time before you drive it (if it is left in an accessible place overnight) for any such devices. I usually place them on the exhaust. I do this to enable me to know where you have been and to allow me to just appear so I can see you and try to establish contact with you once again.

- You need to have your home swept for bugs. In situations where I have not lived with somebody I have established bugs in their home so I am able to listen to you. I will want to know what you are talking about. It is likely that you will be discussing me with friends and family and it will provide me with fuel if I am able to listen in on your conversations. Similarly, to the tracking device and software on your mobile phone I also need to know what you are doing, where and when, so I can make an appearance.

- Have any computers that I had access to, checked by a professional for software that enables me to access it remotely and read for instance your emails and access banking and other information on your computer. If I know you have financial worries, I will seek to exploit that. If I can see you purchasing certain things and receiving email confirmations this will provide me with ideas for gifts that I can send you.

- Repeatedly sending you texts. As above.

- Bombarding you on social media. The most effective response here is not to be on social media. If you cannot do this, then you will need to block me. I will of course use false accounts to try and follow you or friend you and accordingly you need to be vigilant. I will also have certain of those you engage on social media as my Lieutenants feeding me information. You will find rooting those people out rather difficult. Whilst you will be likely to stop me contacting you, you won't stop the flow of information to me which I will use to try and contact you in other ways.

- Be aware I will use technology to try and find out about you and contact you. I will search your name in google to see what can be found there. I may have hacked your Facebook account or you have not been careful enough with your privacy settings, which allows me to save photos of you for my use and discover details about where you have been and who with. With regard to twitpic and flickr you will have left geotags on your images. I know that most people do not bother to turn off the location metadata that is attached to their photos. I will be able to establish where a photo was taken and see if that is your new home or new workplace. I will be able to ascertain which restaurant you are in having just posted the picture and then turn up. If I know that you have your own domain for business purposes I will conduct a whois search and locate your personal details through that. I will utilise Tineye and Google Images to undertake reverse image searches which may yield me information.

- I will use other methods of locating you through electoral rolls, city rates property searches and car licence plate searches. I will maintain that I have been in an accident with your vehicle and you drove away in order to obtain your address details to make a claim from the relevant vehicle licensing authority (and in reality find out where you are)

- I like the fact you upload photos. I will have ensured that when we were together I obtained the exif data from one of the photos that you have uploaded. This data includes the time and date a photo was taken and also a unique serial number. Once I know that number I will be able to locate any photos that you have taken with that camera, anywhere on the internet. Thus I will soon be able to ascertain which are your photos, when you took them and work out locations and people from their contents, even if you do not appear on the photograph. If you used a smartphone to take the photograph, it gets even better as the GPS coordinates will be included. I do know that match.com and plentyoffish.com do remove the gps information from pictures that you upload but there are many websites that do not.

- When you use a copier all of the information that is copied by that machine is recorded on the hard drive of the copier. It is not going to be difficult for me to organise a copy of that hard drive to look through if I wanted to do this. If we work or worked at the same company, then access is easy and even if we do not I will secure access. I am bound to find some information about you that you have copied at work by running the contents of the hard drive through a scanner searching for certain key words.

- You would be well advised to delete all social media applications as it is highly likely that I am viewing your profiles using fake accounts or that I know your passwords and I am thus able to access your accounts and read messages etc. If you cannot live without them, I would recommend that you delete the relevant social media and set up a new account and be extremely careful who you interact with as it may be one of my lieutenants or me in a false guise.

- I will turn up at your house, your workplace, where you shop and where you see friends. I will often just stand and watch so you know that I am there. Over time I will attempt to speak to you and seek to hoover you back in with false promises of changing and doing things right this time. If you are able to, you must get away from me. Do not answer the door. If I cause trouble in some way by being abusive or damaging property you need to call the police. Ultimately you may need to obtain an injunction or restraining order to keep me away from your person.

- Be very wary of engaging in online dating. I may appear in another guise. I will also try to recruit someone to date you and then feed back to me about you. I will also use that person to abuse you by proxy. Don't believe me? I have done this to two different people. I knew from hacking into the relevant girlfriends' Facebook accounts that the two men involved were childhood sweethearts and therefore would be willing to reconnect in some way. I ensured they were appraised of how awful you actually were, I advised the men in question that you had said bad things about them behind their backs (it is not difficult to establish some false e-mails between 'you' and 'a friend' talking about how you are just taking them for a ride and not really interested in them) and a financial incentive does no harm either. By deploying this technique, I was able to perpetuate my campaign against two girlfriends who thought they had escaped me. Be aware this tactic may well be used by your former narcissist. After all, we do tend to think in similar ways don't we?

- I will send gifts to you at home and at work. Do not accept them. Politely decline them and ask for them to be returned by the courier.

- I will engage in a smear campaign and a character assassination in the hope of provoking you into contacting me to challenge me about what I am saying about you. I will do this myself and do it by proxy too, engaging others to propagate lies about you. I know, because you are a decent person that you will want to challenge what I have said because you cannot bear to have untruths told about you. You need to grow a thick skin. For the most part you can ignore the comments. True friends will know I am telling lies. It will not be pleasant but you need to persevere. If the nature of the allegations become serious and repeated you may have to turn to the law to assist, through seeking an injunction or restraining order or even commencing defamation proceedings. Be aware however that by involving the legal process this will bring you into contact with me so you need to think carefully about how you will do this and use a lawyer who is experienced in dealing with people like me.

- I will threaten to hurt myself, lie about having an illness or even threaten suicide if you will not engage with me. Again, because of the caring person you are, I am doing this to appeal to your central beliefs in the hope that you will crumble. You must remain resolute and ignore these protestations. If I do hurt myself, that is my problem and not yours. My kind and me rarely carry out threats of suicide as we actually find doing so contrary to our massive sense of superiority. That is not to say it does not happen, but it is extremely rare. Again, however hard it feels, this was my decision and not yours.

- You must resist any temptation to spy on me. I know how much you want to find out about what I am doing. You know you can look at my Facebook account and there will be no evidence for me to know you have done it, so why not? Every time you look at what I am doing or try and find out through a third party, you are letting me back into your life. This will trigger unpleasant feelings for you and also heightens the risk that your resolve will crumble and you will then fall victim to my attempts to contact you and draw you back in again. I am counting on you lacking the willpower to stay away from checking up on me. That is why I will wait and keep pressing because I know you want to do this. You must never again try and find out about my life in any way. This is often the hardest part because you do not regard it a true contact, but it is a form of contact and one which pulls you down the path towards being sucked into my toxic world again.

- Ditch those friends you know are my Lieutenants and worshippers. You should know by now that they can never be persuaded to think ill of me. You may get along with them still but they will be telling me all about you. They will be mentioning you to me (on my instruction). You may feel you are losing some good things by severing these friendships but they are outweighed by the risks and dangers of maintaining these relationships.

- If you are involved in court proceedings with me be prepared for me to direct all my rage through this. I will repeatedly lie, try to con my lawyer, your lawyer and the judge and other officials involved in the case. I will make agreements with you and then break them. I will make you think that a compromise has been reached and then do the opposite. If you are able to avoid having to engage me through the court process so much the better. If you are left with no choice than to do so you must find a lawyer who has dealt with my kind before (otherwise, you run the risk of not being believed and your lawyer being hoodwinked by my behaviour) and you must be prepared for a difficult and long battle. If the argument is about certain financial matters, you may consider that your sanity is worth more than a little extra money each month. Of course if the financial issue is of necessity and/or the proceedings involve children you will have little option other than to engage. In those circumstances ensure that all communication is through the lawyers. Do not be fooled by me appearing and suggesting that we can try and sort things out between ourselves. I have no interest in doing this. I want the friction to continue as I derive fuel from it. Keep a barrier in place through your lawyer.

- Remove trigger items. Again this is hard and some of them may even be expensive and useful but each time you slip on that Tiffany bracelet remember it is my cold, dead hand gripping your wrist ready to haul you back into my personal hell. Delete the photos and the songs, burn the letters and pictures and sell the gifts. Remember the points I made above about handling Everprescence.

- Fill your time. I play on the fact that you will be sat around reminiscing about our good times. You will keep harking back to that because I know that you will not be able to process intellectually at first and then emotionally (for a very long time and probably forever) that you fell in love with the person you thought I was. This despair means you will turn to memories in order to try and manage the pain. This is dangerous. By clinging to the memories you are not allowing yourself to move on from me. By holding onto those memories you are making yourself want the golden period all the more and with that you run the risk of giving up no contact and returning to me. It is very similar to breaking a relationship with an addictive substance. It is so hard to go without the thing you are trying to give up so that you give in and have a drink even though you know what will ultimately happen. I know this and I will prey on this. Accordingly, you need to find new things to do. This will fill your time and lessen the opportunity for wallowing in nostalgia. It will also distract you and give you something else to focus on. Read all about what you have been through. Read more of my books and remind yourself of how hellish it is and how you do not want to return to it. Do not deny what has happened. Yes, it hurts to experience it and you need to embrace the pain or it will build up and become worse. Knowledge really does empower you.

- Join up to forums and communities that deal with what you have experienced. You will make new friends who entirely understand what has happened to you. You will also find that you are helping others (something as an empathetic individual that comes naturally to you) and the pleasure you gain from doing this will assuage the pain you feel.

- You may find that you have little choice but to change your name, use a PO Box and move to another location to escape the ways that I can track you down in order to try and establish contact with you once again and draw you back into my world.


## Your Vulnerability

Unfortunately for you, you will never be able to completely eradicate me from you. I have achieved this absolutely on purpose. I have shattered your being and your heart and you will repair most of it. You will eventually conquer the shame at being hoodwinked. You will restore your finances and your broken home. You will reduce and extinguish the anxiety and trauma you felt. It will take a long time. It will take effort and discipline but you will get there. You will however not be able to repair your heart entirely. There will always be a small crack, a hairline fracture, a slight puncture hole in it. That is the permanent effect of having danced with me. I know that crack is there and if ever given the chance I will apply my poison so it creeps through that crack, seeps through the fracture and trickles into the hole. From there, it will start to grow and multiply as my toxicity rages through you as it seeks to open you up once more and drag you back to me.

It is a fact that you will always carry this vulnerability. It is part of our design. It is a necessary consequence of how we affect you. This means that you are always at risk from being influenced from us again and that is why you must remain your vigilance and no contact for ever. Do not think after ten years that you can contact me and be safe from my influence. You are always in danger. There is no hope other than to remain away from me.

# Conclusion

Being drawn into my false world is a nightmare existence. Remaining there becomes even worse. The above will equip you with tools to manage and minimise the effect of my behaviour so that you can escape the worst of me. This situation may be the best you can hope for because, for whatever reason, you are not able physically to escape me. Alternatively, these tactics will enable you to then muster sufficient confidence to then look to escape and apply no contact. So long as you maintain this and the principles it engenders you will escape my kind.

You will have noted that I make repeated reference to energy and emotional reactions. We need this fuel. Deprive us of it one way and we will seek it another. Keep blocking us and most of us will find it from someone else, so long as you do not give us a reason to return to you. Most of my kind seeks economy of effort and you must keep that in your mind when applying these techniques. It may take time for the effect to be achieved but it will happen. There are others who will give us our supply and we will look to them instead. You must remain focussed and disciplined.

There are those of us who will keep on and on until you take drastic action by way of effectively making yourself invisible to us or we are restrained in some way (usually prison) from being able to contact you. Those of us who act in such a malign manner are limited in number and you will have to hope that you have not become ensnared in such a web. If you have, you will have to apply these techniques with added vigour, vigilance and know you are in for a rough ride and the long haul. Those types of narcissist are not typical and for the most part using these tactics will make you an unattractive proposition to us and thus we go and hunt down someone else who is appealing to us and who has not acquired the wisdom you have.

Finally, you may wonder why I have done this. Why have I provided you with the insight into the way that I think (and therefore the ways of my brethren)? Surely I wish to keep these secrets and techniques to myself? Not at all, I am delighted to know that people will read what I have written. I am a huge believer in people being allowed to self-determine. We are all adults. Why should you not be furnished with the requisite knowledge to allow you to make an informed decision as to how you live your life and achieve the best outcome? Am I not concerned that this will mean my supply of fuel will be diminished? Not at all. For the good of the world, your kind outnumbers my kind by many and therefore there will always be those who do not heed my writings or do but do not apply the content of them. Furthermore, I enjoy a challenge and by giving you a head start the contest becomes all the more intriguing. Armed with this information you will outflank and escape from many of my kind.

Always remember that escape is attainable. You can do it. Just hope you don't meet me.

Thank you for reading Escape: How To Beat the Narcissist

**Also by HG Tudor**

**Narcissist: Seduction**

**Narcissist: Ensnared**

**Evil**

**Manipulated**

**Confessions of a Narcissist**

**More Confessions of a Narcissist**

**Further Confessions of a Narcissist**

**From the Mouth of a Narcissist**

**Danger : 50 Things You Should Not Do With a Narcissist**

**Departure Imminent: Preparing for No Contact to Beat the Narcissist**

## Engage with HG Tudor

Twitter @narcissist_me

Facebook: Knowing the Narcissist

Blog: Knowing the Narcissist narcsite.wordpress.com

**Forthcoming titles**

**Exposed**

**Lovefraud**

**Narcissist: Unmasked**

**The Girl Next Door**

Made in the USA
Monee, IL
07 May 2023

33275101R00089